GW01314297

Ginger

A Simple Ginger Cookbook with Tasty Ginger Recipes for All Types of Delicious Meals

By
BookSumo Press
All rights reserved

Published by
http://www.booksumo.com

Table of Contents

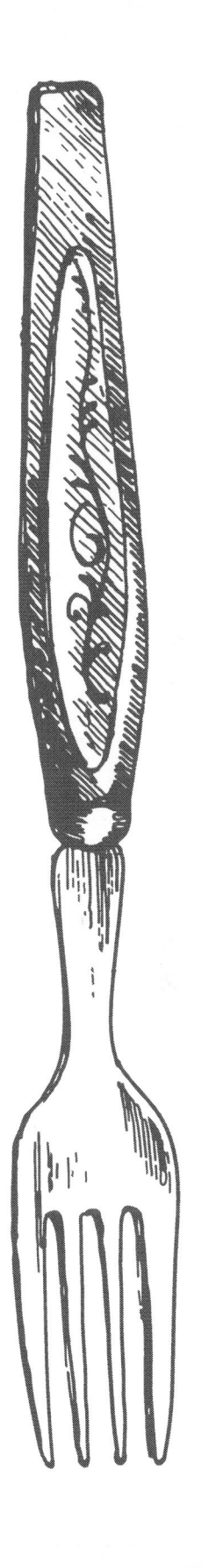

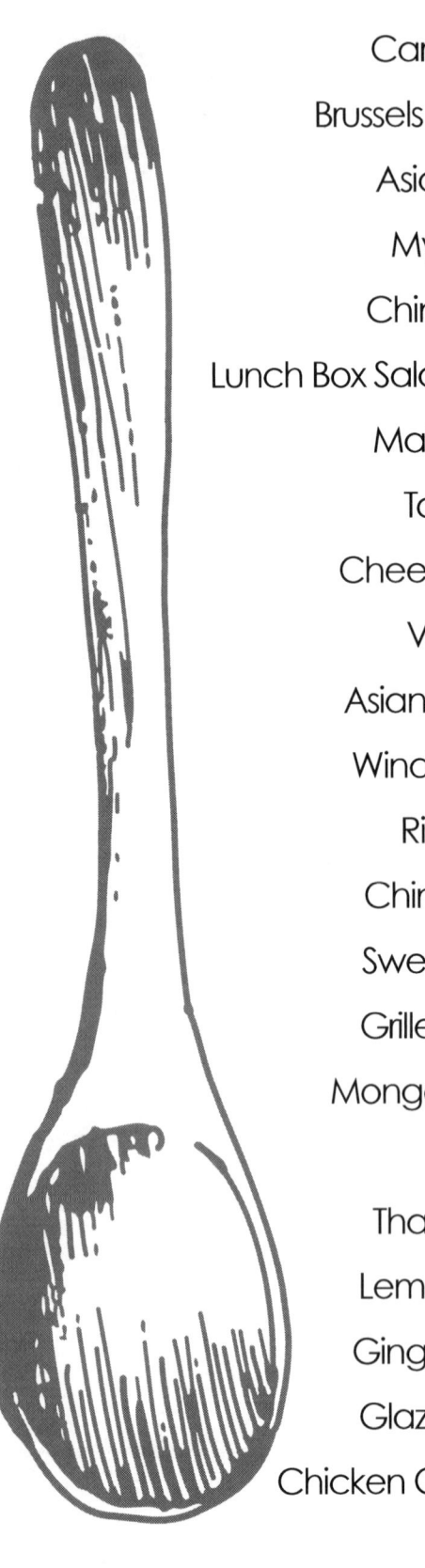

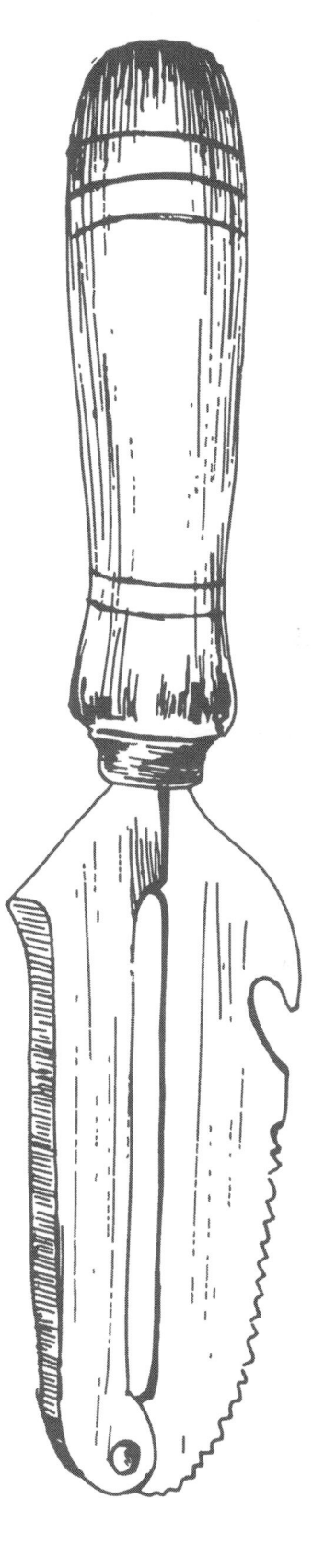

Korean
Beef Skillet

🥣 Prep Time: 15 mins
⏲ Total Time: 30 mins

Servings per Recipe: 2
Calories	944.8 kcal
Fat	30.7 g
Cholesterol	340.2 mg
Sodium	1740.6 mg
Carbohydrates	106.1 g
Protein	58.9 g

Ingredients

1 lb. flank steaks, sliced into strips
3/4 C. cornstarch
1/2 C. water
2 eggs
1 large carrot, julienned
3 green onions, chopped
1/4 C. ginger, minced
5 garlic cloves, minced

canola oil
3 tbsps soy sauce
4 tbsps rice vinegar
1 tbsp sesame oil
1/2 C. sugar
3 tsps crushed red pepper flakes

Directions

1. Place a large pan over medium heat. Heat in it the oil.
2. Get a mixing bowl: Mix in it the water with cornstarch.
3. Add the eggs and whisk them until they become smooth. Stir in the steak slices.
4. Place a pan over medium heat. Heat in it 1 inch of oil. Deep fry in it the beef strips in batches until they become golden.
5. Drain the beef strips and place them aside on paper towels.
6. Drain the oil from the pan leaving 1 tbsp of it. Stir in the carrots, onion, ginger, and garlic.
7. Let them cook for 5 min over high heat. Stir in the vinegar cooked beef strips, with soy sauce, sesame oil, pepper flakes and sugar.
8. Let them cook until they start boiling. Cook them for 1 min.
9. Serve your stir fry right away with some rice.
10. Enjoy..

CHICKEN
Sakong

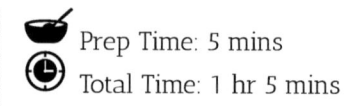

Prep Time: 5 mins
Total Time: 1 hr 5 mins

Servings per Recipe: 4
Calories	174.2 kcal
Fat	3.2 g
Cholesterol	75.5 mg
Sodium	180.8 mg
Carbohydrates	9.9 g
Protein	25.4 g

Ingredients

4 large boneless skinless chicken
breasts
2 tbsps honey
1 -2 tbsp Dijon mustard
4 tbsps water
2 -3 tsps ground ginger

2 -4 garlic cloves, peeled & crushed
salt
ground black pepper

Directions

1. Before you do anything, preheat the oven to 350 F.
2. Get a mixing bowl: Whisk in it the honey, mustard, water, ginger & crushed garlic.
3. Season the chicken breasts with some salt and pepper. Place them in a baking pan.
4. Pour over them the honey sauce and coat them with it. Place it in the oven and let it cook for 1 h.
5. Serve your honey chicken hot with some rice or grilled veggies.
6. Enjoy.

Bronze
Age Cookies

Prep Time: 15 mins
Total Time: 25 mins

Servings per Recipe: 1

Calories	87.5 kcal
Fat	3.5 g
Cholesterol	0.0 mg
Sodium	102.7 mg
Carbohydrates	13.3 g
Protein	0.8 g

Ingredients

3/4 C. margarine, softened
1 C. white sugar
1/4 C. molasses
2 1/2 C. all-purpose flour
1/3 C. water
1 1/2 tsps baking soda
2 tsps ground ginger
1 tsp ground cinnamon

1/2 tsp ground cloves
1/2 tsp allspice
1 tbsp ginger, chopped
1/4 tsp salt
3/4 C. raisins
2 tbsps white sugar

Directions

1. Place a large pan over medium heat. Heat in it the oil.
2. Get a mixing bowl: Beat in it the margarine with 1 C. of sugar until they become smooth and light.
3. Add the molasses and mix them well. Add the baking soda with water and combine them.
4. Mix in the flour with spices and salt until your get a smooth dough. Fold the ginger and raisins into the mixture.
5. Shape the dough into walnut size cookies. Lay them on a greased baking pan.
6. Press them lightly to flaten them. Cook the cookies in the oven for 11 min.
7. Allow them to cool down completely then serve them with some tea.
8. Enjoy.

SAKURA'S
Salad Dressing

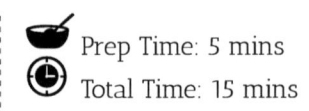
Prep Time: 5 mins
Total Time: 15 mins

Servings per Recipe: 1

Calories	617.4 kcal
Fat	61.9 g
Cholesterol	0.0 mg
Sodium	1631.8 mg
Carbohydrates	16.4 g
Protein	2.5 g

Ingredients

1/2 C. minced onion
1/2 C. peanut oil
1/3 C. rice vinegar
2 tbsps water
2 tbsps minced ginger
2 tbsps minced celery
2 tbsps ketchup

4 tsps soy sauce
2 tsps sugar
2 tsps lemon juice
1/2 tsp minced garlic
1/2 tsp salt
1/4 tsp ground black pepper

Directions

1. Get a food processor: Place in it all the ingredients. Blend them smooth.
2. Place the dressing in the fridge until ready to serve.
3. Enjoy.

Ms. Kim'
Secret Sauce

Prep Time: 15 mins

Total Time: 15 mins

Servings per Recipe: 8

Calories	33.1 kcal
Fat	0.0 g
Cholesterol	0.0 mg
Sodium	2012.5 mg
Carbohydrates	4.2 g
Protein	3.9 g

Ingredients

1 yellow onion, chopped
2 tbsps peeled and grated ginger
1/4 C. lemon juice

1/2 C. white vinegar
1 C. soy sauce

Directions

1. Get a food processor: Place in it all the ingredients. Blend them smooth.
2. Place the dressing in the fridge until ready to serve.
3. Enjoy..

COFFEE
Cakes 101

Prep Time: 20 mins
Total Time: 1 hr

Servings per Recipe: 4
Calories	284.8 kcal
Fat	14.0 g
Cholesterol	10.8 mg
Sodium	241.5 mg
Carbohydrates	38.0 g
Protein	3.2 g

Ingredients

2 1/2 C. flour
3/4 C. sugar
1 C. dark brown sugar
1 tsp salt
1 tsp allspice
3/4 C. Crisco cooking oil
1 beaten egg
1 C. buttermilk

1 tsp baking soda
1 tsp baking powder
2 C. chopped ripe pears
Garnish
1/2 tsp ground ginger
1 C. chopped pecans

Directions

1. Before you do anything, preheat the oven over to 350 F.
2. Get a mixing bowl: Combine in it the flour, sugars, salt, allspice and oil.
3. Place 1 C. of the mixture aside.
4. Mix in 2 C. of chopped pears with egg, buttermilk, baking powder and baking soda to remaining flour mix.
5. Pour the mixture into a greased baking pan. Spread it in an even layer.
6. Get a mixing bowl: Mix in it the remaining 1 C. of flour mix.
7. Add to it the ginger with pecans. Combine them well to make the topping.
8. Sprinkle it on top. Place the pan in the oven and let them cook for 42 min.
9. Serve your crumble warm with some ice cream.
10. Enjoy..

5-Ingredient
Honey Chicken

🥣 Prep Time: 24 hrs
🕐 Total Time: 24 hrs

Servings per Recipe: 4

Calories	350.2 kcal
Fat	0.5 g
Cholesterol	0.0 mg
Sodium	3025.5 mg
Carbohydrates	85.9g
Protein	7.9g

Ingredients

8 -9 chicken pieces, skin on
1 C. honey
3/4 C. soy sauce

1/2 C. minced ginger
1/2 C. minced garlic

Directions

1. Place a saucepan over medium heat. Stir in it the honey, soy sauce, garlic and ginger.
2. Lower the heat and let them cook for 6 min.
3. Place the chicken pieces in a greased pan. Pour the sauce over it.
4. Lay a piece of foil over it to cover it. Place it in the oven and let it cook for 32 min.
5. Once the time is up, discard the foil and turn the heat to 375 F.
6. Flip the chicken pieces and cook them for an extra 35 min. Serve your glazed chicken with some rice.
7. Enjoy..

HOMEMADE
Flavored Yogurt

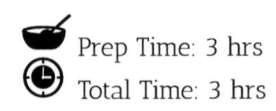

Prep Time: 3 hrs
Total Time: 3 hrs

Servings per Recipe: 4
Calories	126.2 kcal
Fat	2.9 g
Cholesterol	11.9 mg
Sodium	47.4 mg
Carbohydrates	22.4 g
Protein	3.2 g

Ingredients

1 1/2 C. plain yogurt
1/3 C. ginger marmalade
1/3 C. brown sugar

2 tsps lemon juice

Directions

1. Get a mixing bowl: Mix in it all the ingredients.
2. Place your cream dressing in the fridge until ready to serve.
3. Enjoy..

Pacific
Rice

🥣 Prep Time: 5 mins
🕐 Total Time: 25 mins

Servings per Recipe: 6
Calories	141.8 kcal
Fat	1.1 g
Cholesterol	0.0 mg
Sodium	255.2 mg
Carbohydrates	27.8 g
Protein	3.9 g

Ingredients

2 C. chicken broth
1/2 C. reduced-fat coconut milk
2 tsps grated ginger
1 C. uncooked rice
1/2 tsp grated lemon rind

2 green onions, chopped
2 tbsps flaked coconut, toasted
lemon slice

Directions

1. Place a pot over high heat. Stir in it the broth with ginger and coconut milk.
2. Cook them until they start boiling. Add the rice and bring them to another boil.
3. Put on the lid and lower the heat. Let them cook for 16 min.
4. Once the time is up, mix in it the lemon zest with green onions.
5. Serve your rice with a side dish of your choice.
6. Enjoy..

SPICY
Ginger Spaghetti

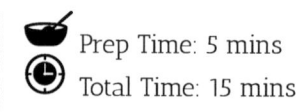
Prep Time: 5 mins
Total Time: 15 mins

Servings per Recipe: 3

Calories	397.9 kcal
Fat	5.5 g
Cholesterol	0.0 mg
Sodium	366.0 mg
Carbohydrates	71.7 g
Protein	16.3 g

Ingredients

8 ounces thin spaghetti
4 green onions, sliced
1/4 C. rice vinegar
2 tbsps low sodium soy sauce
1 - 2 tbsp grated gingerroot
3 tbsps honey

2 tsps sesame oil
1 tsp chili paste
1 tsp toasted sesame seeds

Directions

1. Prepare the pasta by following the instructions on the package. Strain it.
2. Get a mixing bowl: Mix in it the rest of the ingredients. Add the spaghetti and toss them to coat.
3. Adjust the seasoning of your spaghetti then serve it warm.
4. Enjoy..

Min Song's
Favorite Soup

Prep Time: 15 mins
Total Time: 35 mins

Servings per Recipe: 8

Calories	163.1 kcal
Fat	8.1 g
Cholesterol	20.6 mg
Sodium	513.4 mg
Carbohydrates	17.4 g
Protein	5.7 g

Ingredients

1/4 C. butter
2 medium onions, chopped
2 tbsps grated peeled gingerroot
1 1/2 lbs. carrots, peeled and sliced
6 C. chicken stock

1/2 tsp salt
1/2 tsp black pepper

Directions

1. Place a soup pot over medium high heat. Heat in it the butter.
2. Cook in it the onions for 6 min. Stir in the gingerroot and cook them for 3 min.
3. Stir in the stock with carrots. Cook them until they start boiling.
4. Lower the heat and put on the lid. Let them cook for 18 min.
5. Adjust the seasoning of your soup then serve it hot.
6. Enjoy..

ORANGE
Soup

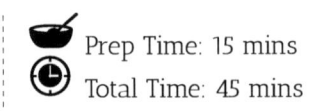 Prep Time: 15 mins
Total Time: 45 mins

Servings per Recipe:

Calories	150.6 kcal
Fat	5.7 g
Cholesterol	13.5 mg
Sodium	146.4 mg
Carbohydrates	24.3 g
Protein	3.0 g

Ingredients

1/16-1/8 C. butter
1 1/2 C. chopped onions
1 tbsp chopped, peeled ginger
1 1/2 tsps minced garlic
1 1/4 lbs. medium carrots, peeled, chopped
2 tomatoes, seeded, chopped

1 1/2 tsps grated lemons, rind
3 C. vegetable stock
2 tbsps lemon juice
4 tbsps sour cream

Directions

1. Place a soup pot over high heat. Cook in it the onion for 5 min.
2. Stir in the ginger with garlic. Cook them for 3 min. Stir in the lemon peel with carrots and tomatoes.
3. Let them cook for 2 min. Stir in 3 C. of stock. Cook them until they start boiling.
4. Lower the heat and put on half a cover. Let them cook for 22 min.
5. Once the time is up, turn off the heat and let the soup cool down for a while.
6. Transfer some of the soup to a food processor and blend it smooth. Repeat the process to blend all the soup.
7. Pour the soup back into the pot. Stir into it the lemon juice with a pinch of salt and pepper.
8. Heat it for 5 min then serve it hot. Garnish it with cream
9. Enjoy..

Sweet
and Sour Broccoli

Prep Time: 10 mins
Total Time: 20 mins

Servings per Recipe: 5

Calories	99.3 kcal
Fat	4.6 g
Cholesterol	0.0 mg
Sodium	649.3 mg
Carbohydrates	12.1 g
Protein	5.0 g

Ingredients

1 1/2 lbs. broccoli, florets and stems sliced into diagonal pieces
1 1/2 tbsps dark sesame oil
3 tbsps soy sauce
1 tbsp ground ginger
2 tsps brown sugar
4 tbsps water

Directions

1. Place a large pan over medium heat. Heat in it the sesame oil
2. Cook in it the broccoli for 9 min.
3. Get a small mixing bowl: Whisk in it the soy sauce, ginger, and sugar. Stir it into the pan with water.
4. Put on the lid and cook them for 3 min. Serve your fried broccoli right away.
5. Enjoy..

EASY
Peking Fish

Prep Time: 10 mins
Total Time: 22 mins

Servings per Recipe: 4
Calories	213.7 kcal
Fat	5.0 g
Cholesterol	51.7 mg
Sodium	88.4 mg
Carbohydrates	18.1 g
Protein	23.1 g

Ingredients

1/3 C. maple syrup
1/3 C. water
1 tbsp ginger, grated
1 garlic clove, chopped
1/4 tsp cayenne pepper, ground

1 (450 g) salmon fillets
salt

Directions

1. Before you do anything, preheat the oven broiler.
2. Season the salt salmon fillets with some salt. Place them aside.
3. Place a large pan over medium heat. Stir in it the rest of the ingredients.
4. Cook them until they start boiling. Let them cook until the sauce reduces by half.
5. Lay the salmon paper on a foil lined up sheet. Place it in the salmon fillets and coat them with the sauce.
6. Place it in the oven and let them cook for 9 min. Serve them warm with some rice or veggies.
7. Enjoy..

How to Make Jasmine Rice

Prep Time: 10 mins
Total Time: 30 mins

Servings per Recipe: 1
Calories	329.4 kcal
Fat	6.3 g
Cholesterol	0.0 mg
Sodium	265.8 mg
Carbohydrates	59.5 g
Protein	7.6 g

Ingredients

3 C. jasmine rice, rinsed and drained
3 tbsps vegetable oil
1/3 C. fresh ginger, chopped, peeled
3 large garlic cloves, minced
4 1/2 C. low sodium chicken broth

3/4 tsp salt
1 bunch fresh cilantro

Directions

1. Place a large saucepan over high heat. Heat in it the oil.
2. Cook in it the garlic with ginger for 35 sec. Stir in the rice and cook them for 4 min.
3. Add the broth with a pinch of salt and cilantro. Cook them until they start boiling.
4. Lower the heat and put on the lid. Let them cook for 20 min.
5. Turn off the heat and let it sit for 12 min. Serve your jasmine rice with your favorite side dish.
6. Enjoy..

THAI
Mushroom Skillet

Prep Time: 10 mins
Total Time: 35 mins

Servings per Recipe: 4
Calories	133.0 kcal
Fat	9.6 g
Cholesterol	0.0 mg
Sodium	512.9 mg
Carbohydrates	8.4 g
Protein	6.7 g

Ingredients

2 tbsps peanut oil
1 1/2 lbs. white button mushrooms,
cleaned quartered
1 tbsp sesame seeds, toasted
1 tbsp ginger, minced
2 tbsps apple cider vinegar

1 tsp sugar
2 tbsps soy sauce
1 tsp toasted sesame oil
2 scallions, sliced

Directions

1. Place a large pan over medium heat. Heat in it 1 tbsp of oil. Cook in it the mushrooms for 6 min.
2. Turn the heat to high and cook them for another 7 min. Stir in the rest of the oil. Cook them for another 7 min.
3. Stir in the sesame seeds with ginger. Cook them for 40 sec.
4. Stir in the rice vinegar, sugar, soy sauce, a pinch of salt and pepper.
5. Cook them for another 40 sec. Garnish your mushrooms with some scallions. Serve them hot.
6. Enjoy..

House
Fried Sirloin

Prep Time: 10 mins
Total Time: 17 mins

Servings per Recipe: 4

Calories	364.8 kcal
Fat	20.7 g
Cholesterol	68.0 mg
Sodium	1597.2 mg
Carbohydrates	15.3 g
Protein	29.0 g

Ingredients

- 6 tbsps soy sauce
- 3 tsps sugar
- 3 tbsps sesame seed oil
- 1 tbsp grated ginger
- 1 lb. boneless beef sirloin, sliced into strips
- 5 tsps sesame oil, divided
- 1 onion, chopped
- 2 cloves garlic, minced
- 2 tsps grated ginger
- 1 C. grated carrot
- 1 red pepper, seeded, and cut into strips
- 2 tsps cornstarch
- 1 tbsp water

Directions

1. Place a large pan over medium heat. Heat in it the oil.
2. Get a mixing bowl: Mix in it all the marinade ingredients. Stir into it the beef strips.
3. Place it aside and let them sit for 35 min.
4. Place a large skillet over medium heat. Heat in it 2 tsp of oil. Cook in it the beef strips for 3 to 4 min.
5. Drain them and place them aside. Heat 3 tsp of oil in the same pan.
6. Cook in it the veggies with ginger and garlic for 2 min. Stir in the cooked beef stripes and cook them for 3 min.
7. Add the cornstarch with water. Mix them well and cook them for 1 to 2 min.
8. Serve your beef stir fry warm with some rice.
9. Enjoy..

TERRIFIC
Teriyaki Burgers

Prep Time: 15 mins
Total Time: 25 mins

Servings per Recipe: 4
Calories	633.0 kcal
Fat	28.8 g
Cholesterol	176.0 mg
Sodium	2815.4 mg
Carbohydrates	58.1 g
Protein	36.2 g

Ingredients

1 1/4 lbs. ground chicken
2/3 C. panko breadcrumbs
1 egg, lightly beaten
2 green onions, sliced
3 tbsps chopped cilantro
1 clove garlic, minced
1 tsp Asian hot chili sauce
1 tsp salt
1 tbsp vegetable oil
1/2 C. bottled teriyaki sauce
4 tsps honey
4 hamburger buns with sesame seeds,
split and toasted
4 leaves red leaf lettuce
1 cucumber, peeled, seeded, halved and
sliced lengthwise
Cream
1/2 C. mayonnaise
2 tsps sweet pickle relish
2 tsps minced ginger
2 tsps lime juice
1 clove garlic, minced
1/4 tsp salt

Directions

1. To prepare the ginger cream:
2. Get a mixing bowl: Whisk in it all the ginger cream ingredients.
3. Place the cream in the fridge until ready to serve.
4. To prepare the chicken:
5. Get a mixing bowl: Combine in it the chicken, panko, egg, onions, cilantro, garlic, chili sauce and salt.
6. Shape the mixture into 4 burgers.
7. Get a small mixing bowl: Whisk in it the honey with teriyaki glaze. Coat the burgers with the mixture.
8. Place a large pan over medium heat. Heat in it 1 tbsp of oil. Cook in it the burgers for 4 to 6 min on each side.
9. Assemble your burgers and place the way you desire with the ginger cream.
10. Serve your burgers right away.
11. Enjoy..

Muffins
Chiang Mai

Servings per Recipe: 1

Calories	168.2 kcal
Fat	6.3 g
Cholesterol	15.9 mg
Sodium	320.7 mg
Carbohydrates	25.5 g
Protein	2.7 g

Ingredients

1 1/2 C. sifted all-purpose flour
1 3/4 tsps baking powder
1/2 tsp baking soda
1/2 tsp salt
3/4 tsp ground ginger
1/2 tsp ground cinnamon
1/2 tsp ground cloves
6 tbsps margarine, softened

1/3 C. granulated sugar
1/3 C. packed light brown sugar
1 egg
2/3 C. canned pumpkin
1/2 C. buttermilk
1/2 C. chopped crystallized ginger

Directions

1. Before you do anything, preheat the oven to 350 F.
2. Line up a muffin pan with muffin cups.
3. Place a large pan over medium heat. Heat in it the oil.
4. Get a mixing bowl: Mix in it the flour, baking powder, baking soda, salt, ginger, cinnamon, and cloves.
5. Get a large mixing bowl: Cream in it the margarine, granulated sugar, and brown sugar until they become smooth.
6. Add the egg with pumpkin. Mix them until they become creamy. Mix in the flour gradually with milk.
7. Combine them well. Stir the ginger into the batter. Pour the batter into the muffin cups.
8. Cook them in the oven for 28 min.
9. Allow your muffins to cool down completely. Serve them with your favorite toppings.
10. Enjoy..

DARK
Stir Fried Peas

Prep Time: 10 mins
Total Time: 20 mins

Servings per Recipe: 4
Calories	83.5 kcal
Fat	6.8 g
Cholesterol	0.0 mg
Sodium	253.4 mg
Carbohydrates	4.0 g
Protein	1.8 g

Ingredients

1 tbsp peanut oil
1 tsp ginger, peeled and minced
2 C. snow peas
1 tbsp soy sauce
1 tbsp dark sesame oil

salt
black pepper

Directions

1. Place a large pan over medium high heat. Heat in it the peanut oil. Cook in it the ginger with peas for 3 min.
2. Stir in the soy sauce. Turn off the heat and spoon the mixture to a serving plate.
3. Heat the sesame oil in the same pan for 15 sec. Drizzle it over the peas salad.
4. Serve it right away with your favorite toppings.
5. Enjoy..

Cambodian
Chicken Griller

🥘 Prep Time: 5 mins
🕐 Total Time: 20 mins

Servings per Recipe: 4
Calories   358.7 kcal
Fat   11.8 g
Cholesterol   69.6 mg
Sodium   2081.7 mg
Carbohydrates   38.1 g
Protein   27.2 g

Ingredients

1/2 C. soy sauce
1/2 C. honey
1 tbsp roasted sesame seeds

3 tsps ginger, minced
3 - 4 chicken breasts

Directions

1. Before you do anything, preheat the grill and grease it.
2. Get a mixing bowl: Whisk in it the soy sauce, honey, sesame seeds, and ginger.
3. Coat the chicken breasts with the ginger mixture. Place them on the grill.
4. Cook the chicken breasts for 7 to 9 min on each side. Serve them warm.
5. Enjoy..

OCTOBER
Pancakes with Flavored Butter

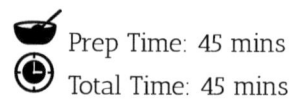

Prep Time: 45 mins
Total Time: 45 mins

Servings per Recipe: 1
Calories	183.9 kcal
Fat	10.4 g
Cholesterol	49.8 mg
Sodium	354.8 mg
Carbohydrates	19.2 g
Protein	3.9 g

Ingredients

Pancakes
1 C. flour
2 tbsps packed brown sugar
1 tsp baking powder
1/2 tsp baking soda
1/2 tsp ground cinnamon
1/2 tsp ground ginger
1/4 tsp allspice
1/4 tsp salt
1 large egg

3/4 C. milk
3/4 C. canned pumpkin
1/4 C. plain low-fat yogurt
2 tbsps melted butter
Butter
2 tbsps chopped candied ginger
1/4 C. softened butter

Directions

1. Place a large pan over medium heat. Heat in it the oil.
2. Get a mixing bowl: Stir in it the flour, brown sugar, soda, and cinnamon, powdered ginger, allspice and salt.
3. Get a mixing bowl: Whisk in it the egg, milk pumpkin, yogurt and butter.
4. Add it to the flour mix and combine them well.
5. Place a griddle pan over medium heat. Grease it with some butter.
6. Pour in it a some of the pancake batter then cook it for 1 to 2 min on each side.
7. Get a mixing bowl: Beat in it the candied ginger with butter until they become smooth.
8. Serve your pancakes warm with your butter ginger.
9. Enjoy..

Maui
Maui Salmon

🥣 Prep Time: 5 mins
🕐 Total Time: 20 mins

Servings per Recipe: 4
Calories	435.6 kcal
Fat	15.0 g
Cholesterol	78.4 mg
Sodium	3589.9 mg
Carbohydrates	32.2 g
Protein	46.1 g

Ingredients

1/3 C. orange juice
1/3 C. soy sauce
1/4 C. honey
1 tbsp Dijon mustard
1 inch ginger, chopped

2 garlic cloves, minced
3 green onions, chopped
1 1/2 lbs. salmon fillets

Directions

1. Season the salmon fillets with some salt and pepper.
2. Get a roasting pan: Mix in it the rest of the ingredients.
3. Add to it the fish fillets and coat them with the sauce mixture. Let them sit for 20 min.
4. Before you do anything, preheat the grill and grease it.
5. Drain the salmon fillets and cook them on the grill for 5 to 7 min on each side.
6. Baste the fillets of the with the remaining sauce. Serve them warm with your favorite toppings.
7. Enjoy..

DIJON
Ginger Fillets

Prep Time: 10 mins
Total Time: 20 mins

Servings per Recipe: 4
Calories	272.9 kcal
Fat	7.7 g
Cholesterol	77.4 mg
Sodium	506.1 mg
Carbohydrates	14.3 g
Protein	34.9 g

Ingredients

1/4 C. packed brown sugar
2 tbsps Dijon mustard
1 tbsp grated ginger
4 (6 ounce) salmon fillets, skinned

1/2 tsp salt
1/2 tsp ground black pepper

Directions

1. Before you do anything, preheat the grill and grease it.
2. Season the salmon fillets with salt and pepper.
3. Get a mixing bowl: Mix in it the sugar with ginger and mustard.
4. Coat the salmon fillets with the mixture.
5. Place them on the grill and let them cook for 6 to 8 min on each side.
6. Serve your grilled salmon fillet with your favorite toppings.
7. Enjoy..

Ms. Chow's
Ginger Dressing

Prep Time: 10 mins
Total Time: 10 mins

Servings per Recipe: 5

Calories	102.3 kcal
Fat	8.8 g
Cholesterol	0.0 mg
Sodium	401.2 mg
Carbohydrates	5.0 g
Protein	1.4 g

Ingredients

2 tbsps peanut oil
1/4 C. rice vinegar
3 tbsps white miso
1 tbsp dark sesame oil
2 medium carrots, peeled and cut into pieces
1 inch gingerroot, peeled and cut into coins
1 - 2 tsp sugar
salt and peppe

Directions

1. Get a blender: Place it in it thee oil with vinegar, miso, sesame oil, carrot, gingerroot and sugar.
2. Blend them smooth. Add a pinch of salt and pepper and combine them well.
3. Place the ginger dressing in the fridge until ready to serve.
4. Enjoy..

BALSAMIC
Salad

Prep Time: 15 mins
Total Time: 1 hr 5 mins

Servings per Recipe: 4

Calories	158.3 kcal
Fat	5.5 g
Cholesterol	0.0 mg
Sodium	177.5 mg
Carbohydrates	25.4 g
Protein	4.0 g

Ingredients

2 lbs. beets, cleaned and trimmed
1 1/2 tbsps extra virgin olive oil
1 1/2 tbsps finely grated ginger
2 tbsps balsamic vinegar

salt
pepper

Directions

1. Before you do anything, preheat the oven to 375 F.
2. Place each beef in a piece of foil and wrap it around it.
3. Place the wrapped beets on a baking sheet. Cook them in the oven for 45 min to 1 h until they become soft.
4. Open the foil packets and let the beets cool down completely.
5. Peel the beets and slice them.
6. Place a pan over medium heat. Heat in it the oil. Cook in it the ginger for 1 min.
7. Stir in the beets and increase the heat. Cook them for 4 min. Stir in the vinegar with a pinch of salt.
8. Cook them for 1 min. Serve your warm beet salad warm.
9. Enjoy..

Hawaiian
Fish Roast

Prep Time: 10 mins
Total Time: 25 mins

Servings per Recipe: 4

Calories	178.5 kcal
Fat	3.5 g
Cholesterol	114.9 mg
Sodium	618.6 mg
Carbohydrates	2.4 g
Protein	32.3 g

Ingredients

4 (6 ounce) white fish fillets
1 C. boiling water
1 chicken bouillon cube
3 large scallions, sliced
1 piece ginger, peeled, cut into matchsticks
1/4 tsp cayenne pepper
1 tbsp soy sauce

1 tbsp apple cider vinegar
1 tsp cornstarch
2 tbsps water
1 tsp olive oil
salt and pepper

Directions

1. Before you do anything, preheat the oven to 425 F.
2. Get 1 C. of boiling water: Stir into it a chicken bouillon until it dissolves.
3. Season the fish fillets with cayenne pepper, salt and pepper.
4. Place them in a roasting dish and pour over them 1/4 C. of the bouillon mix.
5. Sprinkle the green onion slices on top. Lay over it a piece of foil to cover it.
6. Place the pan in the oven and let it cook for 1 min.
7. Get a mixing bowl: Whisk in it the rest of the bouillon mix with soy sauce, apple cider vinegar, cornstarch and 2 tbsp water.
8. Place a frying pan over medium heat. Heat in it the olive oil. Cook in it the white scallion parts then cook them for 2 min.
9. Stir in it the cornstarch mixture and bring them to a boil. Cook them until the sauce becomes thick.
10. Transfer fish fillets into serving plates. Spoon the sauce over them then serve them hot.
11. Enjoy..

GLAZED
Alaskan Salmon

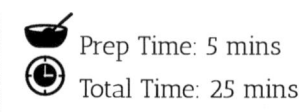

Prep Time: 5 mins
Total Time: 25 mins

Servings per Recipe: 4

Calories	309.9 kcal
Fat	7.6 g
Cholesterol	78.4 mg
Sodium	1469.4 mg
Carbohydrates	22.1 g
Protein	37.9 g

Ingredients

1 tsp ginger
1 tsp garlic powder
1/3 C. soy sauce
1/3 C. orange juice
1/4 C. honey

1 green onion, chopped
1 1/2 lbs. salmon fillets

Directions

1. Before you do anything, preheat the grill and grease it.
2. Get a mixing bowl: Mix in it the ginger with garlic powder, soy sauce, orange juice and honey.
3. Season the salmon fillets with some salt and pepper.
4. Cook them on the grill for 5 to 8 min on each side while basting them with the ginger sauce.
5. Transfer your grilled salmon to serving plates. Garnish them with green onions then serve them.
6. Enjoy..

Calgary
Cinnamon Cookies

🥣 Prep Time: 10 mins
🕐 Total Time: 30 mins

Servings per Recipe: 1
Calories	148.1 kcal
Fat	1.6 g
Cholesterol	0.0 mg
Sodium	162.0 mg
Carbohydrates	30.1 g
Protein	4.4 g

Ingredients

2 bananas
1/2 C. molasses
2 tsps vanilla
1 C. whole wheat flour
2 C. oats

2 tsps baking soda
1 tsp ginger
3 tsps cinnamon

Directions

1. Before you do anything, preheat the oven to 350 F.
2. Get a mixing bowl: Combine in it all the ingredients well.
3. Spoon mounds of the dough into a greased baking pan. Cook them in the oven for 22 to 26 min.
4. Allow the cookies to cool down completely. Serve them with some tea.
5. Enjoy..

GINGERROOT
Soup

Prep Time: 20 mins
Total Time: 1 hr

Servings per Recipe: 4

Calories	128.3 kcal
Fat	4.2 g
Cholesterol	42.6 mg
Sodium	512.3 mg
Carbohydrates	10.9 g
Protein	13.1 g

Ingredients

1 tsp olive oil
2 garlic cloves, minced
1 tbsp gingerroot, peeled and minced
1 tsp lemon peel, grated
1/4 tsp dried red pepper flakes
4 C. low sodium chicken broth
1 tbsp low sodium soy sauce
1 tbsp lemon juice

3 carrots, peeled and sliced
1/4 lb. scallops, diced
1/4 lb. large shrimp, peeled and diced
1 tsp sesame oil
4 green onions, chopped
2 tbsps cilantro, chopped

Directions

1. Place a soup pot over medium heat. Heat in it the oil.
2. Cook in it the garlic, ginger, lemon peel and hot pepper flakes for 1 min.
3. Stir in the broth, soy sauce and lemon juice. Cook them until they start boiling.
4. Stir in the carrots and lower the heat. Let them cook for 16 min.
5. Stir in the scallops, shrimp, sesame oil and green onions. Let them cook for 5 min.
6. Serve your sea soup hot. Garnish it with cilantro.
7. Enjoy..

Pacific
Kabobs I (Beef)

🥣 Prep Time: 10 mins
🕐 Total Time: 24 hrs 18 mins

Servings per Recipe: 10
Calories	510.0 kcal
Fat	36.9 g
Cholesterol	91.1 mg
Sodium	879.5 mg
Carbohydrates	16.4 g
Protein	28.4 g

Ingredients

1/2 C. soy sauce
3 - 4 tbsps honey
2 tbsps white vinegar
1 1/2 tsps garlic powder
1 1/2 tsps ginger powder
3/4 C. oil
1 green onion, chopped
3 lbs. boneless beef sirloin, cubed

1 large fresh pineapple, peeled, cored and cut into chunks
3 green bell peppers, cut into pieces
2 red onions, cut into pieces
10 long metal skewers

Directions

1. Place a large pan over medium heat. Heat in it the oil.
2. Get a mixing bowl: Whisk in it the soy sauce, honey, vinegar, ginger, garlic, oil and green onion to make the marinade.
3. Get a roasting dish: Stir in it the marinade with beef cubes. Cover it and let it sit for an overnight in the fridge.
4. Before you do anything else, preheat the grill and grease it.
5. Drain the beef cubes and thread them into the skewers with pineapple and veggies.
6. Place them over the grill and let them cook for 19 to 21 min.
7. Serve your beef kabobs hot with some pita bread.
8. Enjoy..

PACIFIC
Kabobs II (Shrimp)

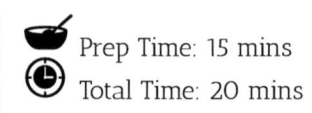

Prep Time: 15 mins
Total Time: 20 mins

Servings per Recipe: 6
Calories	337.2 kcal
Fat	19.8 g
Cholesterol	190.9 mg
Sodium	2373.9 mg
Carbohydrates	16.8 g
Protein	23.8 g

Ingredients

2 lbs. large shrimp, peeled and deveined
Marinade
1/2 C. canola oil
1/2 C. soy sauce
2 tbsps lemon juice
2 tsps grated ginger
4 cloves garlic, minced
Sauce
1/3 C. apricot preserves

1 - 4 tbsp soy sauce
1/4 C. lemon juice
1/2 tsp grated ginger
1 tsp cornstarch
1 tbsp orange juice

Directions

1. Place a large pan over medium heat. Heat in it the oil.
2. Get a mixing bowl: Mix in it the marinade ingredients. Add to it the shrimp.
3. Cover it with a cling foil and let it sit in the fridge for 8 h.
4. Before you do anything else, preheat the grill and grease it.
5. Drain the shrimp and thread it into skewers. Place them on the grill and let them cook for 3 to 4 min on each side.
6. Place a heavy saucepan over medium heat. Stir in it the apricot preserves, soy sauce, lemon juice and 1/2 tsp grated ginger.
7. Cook them until they start boiling. Stir in the cornstarch and cook them until it becomes thick.
8. Serve your apricot sauce warm with the grill shrimp.
9. Enjoy.

Hot
Garbanzo Salad

Prep Time: 5 mins
Total Time: 15 mins

Servings per Recipe: 4

Calories	424.8 kcal
Fat	19.4 g
Cholesterol	0.0 mg
Sodium	637.9 mg
Carbohydrates	53.7 g
Protein	11.0 g

Ingredients

5 tbsps virgin olive oil
1 large red onion, chopped
2 garlic cloves, crushed
2 (15 ounce) cans chickpeas, drained &
rinsed
1/2 tsp powdered ginger
1 pinch dried chili pepper flakes
1 1/2 lemon, juice

1 - 2 tbsp fresh cilantro, chopped
salt and pepper, to taste
1/4 tsp cumin
1/4 tsp paprika

Directions

1. Place a large pan over medium heat. Heat in it 1 tbsp of oil.
2. Cook in it the garlic with onion for 6 min. Stir in the chickpeas, ginger, and chili flakes.
3. Cook them for 40 sec. Stir in the lemon juice and cook them for 2 min.
4. Add the cilantro with a pinch of salt and pepper.
5. Serve your herbed chickpea warm with some pita bread.
6. Enjoy..

HOUSE
Roasted Steak

Prep Time: 15 mins
Total Time: 30 mins

Servings per Recipe: 6
Calories	194.4 kcal
Fat	6.3 g
Cholesterol	31.0 mg
Sodium	934.8 mg
Carbohydrates	17.0 g
Protein	17.8 g

Ingredients

1/3 C. soy sauce
1/3 C. honey
1 tbsp minced garlic
1 tbsp grated gingerroot

1 - 2 lb. flank steak

Directions

1. Use a wooden skewer to poke the several holes in the steak. Season it with some salt and pepper.
2. Get a mixing bowl: Whisk in it the rest of the ingredients to make the sauce.
3. Place the steak in a roasting pan. Pour over it the sauce and coat it with it.
4. Cover it and place it in the fridge for 8 h.
5. Before you do anything else, preheat the grill and grease it.
6. Cook in it the steak for 4 to 6 min on each side. Serve it hot.
7. Enjoy..

Sesame
Kale Skillet

Prep Time: 5 mins

Total Time: 9 mins

Servings per Recipe: 1

Calories	125.3 kcal
Fat	7.6 g
Cholesterol	0.0 mg
Sodium	386.6 mg
Carbohydrates	12.7 g
Protein	4.4 g

Ingredients

1 tbsp minced gingerroot
1/2 tbsp safflower oil
1/4 lb. kale, chopped
1 tsp soy sauce

1/4 C. water
1 tsp toasted sesame seeds

Directions

1. Place a large pan over medium heat. Heat in it the oil. Cook in it the gingerroot for 60 sec.
2. Stir in the kale with soy sauce and water. Cook them over high heat for 3 to 4 min.
3. Stir in the sesame seeds then serve your kake right away.
4. Enjoy..

THAI
Chicken Skillet

Prep Time: 15 mins
Total Time: 30 mins

Servings per Recipe: 4
Calories   336.1 kcal
Fat   14.8 g
Cholesterol   108.9 mg
Sodium   1416.0 mg
Carbohydrates   10.6 g
Protein   39.4 g

Ingredients

3 tbsps peanut oil
1 onion, cut into slivers
6 cloves garlic, minced
1 1/2 lbs. boneless skinless chicken breasts, cubed
2 tbsps soy sauce
2 tbsps chopped gingerroot
2 tbsps chopped mint leaves
8 shiitake mushrooms, stemmed and sliced

5 green onions, chopped into pieces
Thai red chili pepper, slivered
2 tbsps rice vinegar
1 tsp brown sugar
2 tbsps fish sauce
steamed jasmine rice

Directions

1. Get a mixing bowl: Whisk in it the vinegar, fish sauce and brown sugar.
2. Place a large pan over medium heat. Heat in it the oil. Cook in it the onion with chicken and garlic for 3 min.
3. Stir in the soy sauce, ginger, mint, mushrooms, green onions, and chilies. Cook them for 5 min.
4. Stir in the vinegar mixture. Turn off the heat then serve your sweet chicken hot with rice.
5. Enjoy..

Dragon Masters Prawns

Prep Time: 40 mins
Total Time: 50 mins

Servings per Recipe: 4
Calories   289.5 kcal
Fat   10.3 g
Cholesterol   316.8 mg
Sodium   2008.6 mg
Carbohydrates   10.6 g
Protein   37.5 g

Ingredients

2 tbsps vegetable oil
1 kg prawns
1 tbsp garlic, minced
2 tbsps ginger, chopped
1 red chile, chopped
1 C. chicken stock
2 tbsps light soy sauce
4 spring onions
1 tsp corn flour
1 tbsp water

1/8 C. basil leaves, chopped
1/8 C. oregano leaves, chopped
steamed rice

Directions

1. Get a mixing bowl: Whisk in it the corn flour with water. Place it aside.
2. Place a large pan over medium heat. Heat in it the oil.
3. Cook in it the prawns, garlic, ginger and chili for 3 min. Drain the prawns and place them aside.
4. Stir the stock into the pan. Heat it until it starts boiling. Stir in the soy sauce with cornstarch mix.
5. Cook them until they become thick. Stir in the spring onions with cooked prawns. Cook them for 2 min.
6. Serve your ginger prawns hot with some rice.
7. Enjoy..

HAPPY
11 Penne Pasta

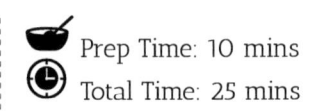

Prep Time: 10 mins
Total Time: 25 mins

Servings per Recipe: 4
Calories	474.4 kcal
Fat	15.7 g
Cholesterol	0.0 mg
Sodium	286.1 mg
Carbohydrates	77.9 g
Protein	8.4 g

Ingredients

1/4 C. vegetable stock
1 tbsp soy sauce
1 tbsp balsamic vinegar
1 tbsp cornstarch
2 garlic cloves, minced
1 tbsp grated ginger
4 tbsps olive oil
3 C. cooked penne pasta

2 onions, sliced
2 carrots, sliced
1 red bell pepper, julienned
1 C. broccoli floret
1/4 tsp dark sesame oil
2 scallions, minced

Directions

1. Place a large saucepan over medium heat. Heat in it 1 tsp of oil.
2. Cook in it the pasta for 3 min. Drain it and place it aside.
3. Heat the rest of the oil in the pan. Cook in it the shallots, carrots, red bell pepper and broccoli for 6 min.
4. Get a mixing bowl: Whisk in it the stock, soy sauce, balsamic vinegar, cornstarch, garlic and ginger.
5. Add it to the pan and let them cook for 3 min. Stir in the pasta with scallions, sesame oil, a pinch of salt and pepper.
6. Serve your stir fry hot.
7. Enjoy..

Country Squash

🥣 Prep Time: 8 mins

🕐 Total Time: 18 mins

Servings per Recipe: 4

Calories	136.9 kcal
Fat	0.2 g
Cholesterol	0.0 mg
Sodium	11.7 mg
Carbohydrates	35.5 g
Protein	2.8 g

Ingredients

2 1/2 lbs. butternut squash, halved and seeded

2 tsps maple syrup

3/4 tsp grated peeled ginger

Directions

1. Wrap the squash halves in a piece of foil. Microwave them for 8 min on high until they become tender.
2. Discard the foil and place them aside to cool down.
3. Use a fork to scrap the squash flesh into a bowl.
4. Mix into it the syrup, ginger and salt and pepper. Serve your spaghetti squash warm.
5. Enjoy..

BUTTERMILK
Cake

Prep Time: 15 mins
Total Time: 1 hr 30 mins

Servings per Recipe: 12
Calories	425.5 kcal
Fat	17.1 g
Cholesterol	94.3 mg
Sodium	250.4 mg
Carbohydrates	64.5 g
Protein	5.8 g

Ingredients

The juice of 2 lemons
The zest of 2 lemons
1 -2 tsp grated ginger
3 C. sifted flour
3/4 tsp baking soda
3/4 tsp baking powder

1 -2 tsp white pepper
1 C. butter
2 1/4 C. sugar, divided
3 eggs
1 C. buttermilk

Directions

1. To prepare the cake:
2. Before you do anything, preheat the oven to 325 F. Place the rack on the third part of the oven.
3. Grease a cake pan with some butter and flour. Place it aside.
4. Get a mixing bowl: Stir in it the flour, baking soda, baking powder and pepper.
5. Get a large mixing bowl: Cream in it the butter until it become smooth.
6. Add to it 3/4 C. of flour and cream them until they become light. Mix in the eggs gradually.
7. Add the buttermilk with flour gradually while alternating between them and mix them at the same time.
8. Get a small bowl: Stir in it the ginger with lemon zest and 2 tbsp of lemon juice.
9. Add it to the batter and mix them well. Pour the mixture into the greased pan.
10. Place it in the oven and let it cook for 75 min.
11. Allow it to cool down completely.
12. To prepare the syrup:
13. Add enough water to the lemon juice until it totals 1/3 cup.
14. Place a heavy saucepan over medium heat: Mix in it the lemon juice with 1/2 C. of sugar.

15. Bring them to a boil then turn off the heat and let them cool down.
16. Coat the whole cake with the lemon syrup then serve it with your favorite toppings.
17. Enjoy..

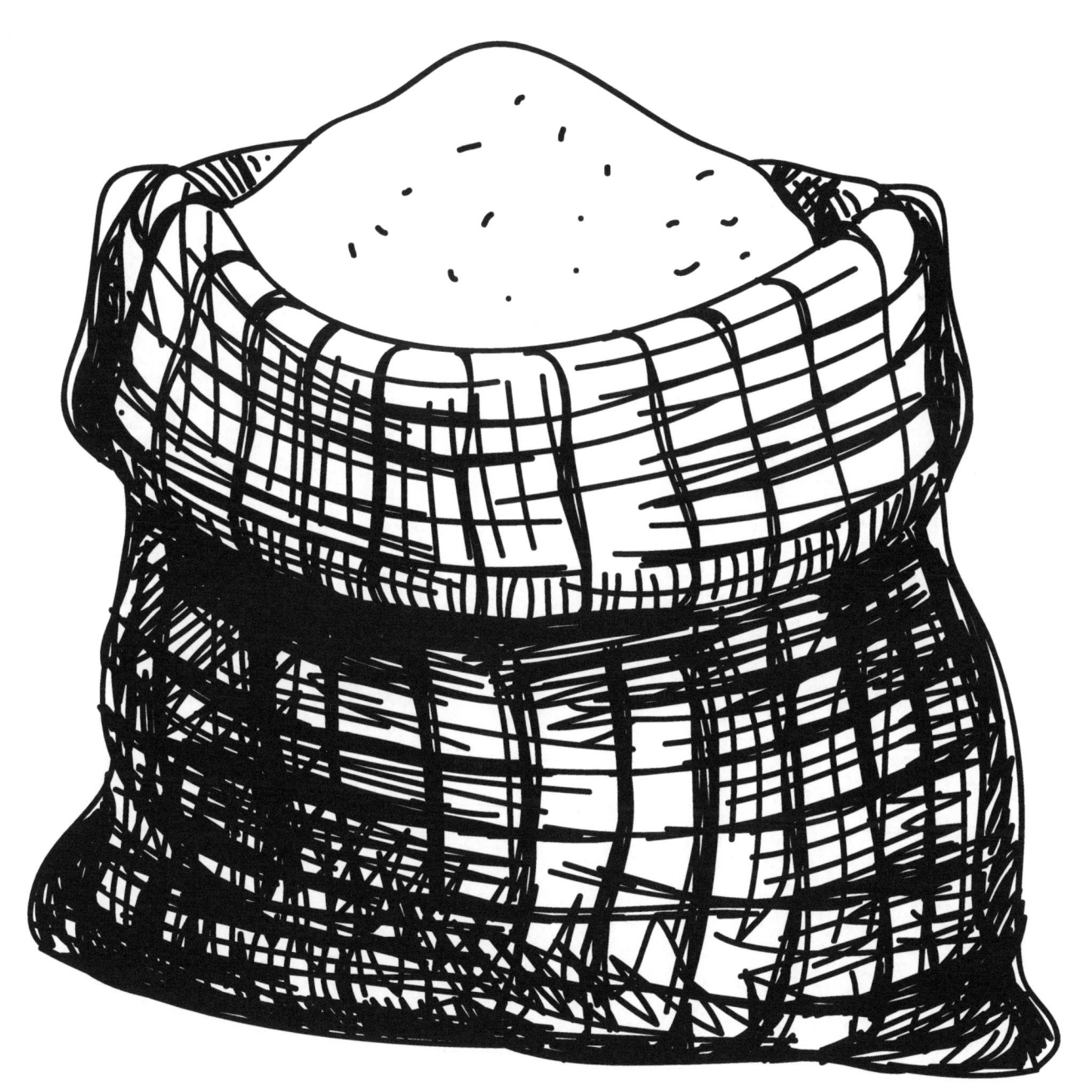

GARDEN
Style Chicken Breasts

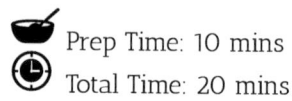

Prep Time: 10 mins
Total Time: 20 mins

Servings per Recipe: 4
Calories	157.0 kcal
Fat	5.3 g
Cholesterol	72.6 mg
Sodium	133.1 mg
Carbohydrates	1.6 g
Protein	24.3 g

Ingredients

1 lb. boneless skinless chicken breast
2 tbsps lemon juice
2 tsps ginger, minced
3 garlic cloves, minced
2 tsps lite olive oil

1 tsp cumin
salt and pepper

Directions

1. Before you do anything, preheat the grill and grease it.
2. Place the chicken breasts between 2 wax sheets.
3. Flatten them with a kitchen hammer or pan until they become 1/2 inch thick.
4. Get a mixing bowl: Whisk in it the lemon juice, ginger, garlic, oil and cumin.
5. Coat the chicken breasts with the mixture. Let them sit for 15 min.
6. Grill the chicken breasts for 3 to 5 min on each side. Serve them hot.
7. Enjoy..

Autumnal
Mashed Potatoes

🥣 Prep Time: 10 mins
🕐 Total Time: 30 mins

Servings per Recipe: 2
Calories   192.5 kcal
Fat   5.8 g
Cholesterol   15.2 mg
Sodium   124.7 mg
Carbohydrates   33.7 g
Protein   2.1 g

Ingredients

2 large kumara, peeled and chopped
1 1/2 tbsps ginger, peeled and grated
1 tbsp brown sugar
1 tbsp butter

salt
white pepper

Directions

1. Place a large salted saucepan of water over medium heat. Cook in it the sweet potatoes until they become soft.
2. Drain them and let them cool down for a while.
3. Get a mixing bowl: Mash in it the sweet potatoes with brown sugar, butter and ginger until they become smooth.
4. Sprinkle over them some salt and pepper. Combine them well.
5. Serve your sweet potato mash right away.
6. Enjoy..

WEST
African Ginger Florets Soup

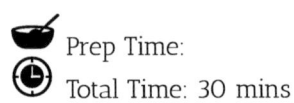

Prep Time:
Total Time: 30 mins

Servings per Recipe: 4
Calories	251.2 kcal
Fat	17.5 g
Cholesterol	0.0 mg
Sodium	329.2 mg
Carbohydrates	19.7 g
Protein	9.0 g

Ingredients

1 1/2 C. broccoli, chopped
1 1/2 C. cauliflower, chopped
1 medium onion, chopped
1 tbsp ginger, grated
3 cloves garlic, chopped
1/4 tsp cayenne pepper
1/2 tsp salt

1/2 tsp pepper
2 tbsps olive oil
3 C. vegetable stock
1 (28 ounce) cans diced tomatoes
5 tbsps natural-style peanut butter

Directions

1. Place a large pot over medium heat. Heat in it the oil.
2. Cook in it the broccoli, cauliflower, onions, ginger, garlic, cayenne, salt, and pepper for 4 min.
3. Stir in the stock, tomatoes, and peanut butter.
4. Lower the heat and let them cook for 22 min.
5. Adjust the seasoning of your soup then serve it hot.
6. Enjoy..

Ginger
Soup Septembers

🥣 Prep Time: 10 mins
🕐 Total Time: 30 mins

Servings per Recipe: 4

Calories	200.1 kcal
Fat	11.7 g
Cholesterol	0.0 mg
Sodium	44.8 mg
Carbohydrates	25.1 g
Protein	3.0 g

Ingredients

20 oz. diced butternut pumpkin
1 large onion, chopped
1 tbsp oil
2 tsps minced garlic
2 tbsps grated gingerroot
1 1/2 C. vegetable stock
1/2 C. coconut milk

1 tbsp lemon juice
1 tbsp tomato paste
1 tsp sugar

Directions

1. Place a soup pot over medium heat. Heat in it the oil.
2. Cook in it the pumpkin, garlic, ginger and onion for 3 min.
3. Stir in the stock and cook them until they start boiling.
4. Lower the heat and cook them for 20 min.
5. Once the time is up, turn off the heat and allow the soup to cool down.
6. Transfer it to a blender and blend it smooth.
7. Pour the soup back into the pot. Stir into it the coconut cream, lemon juice, tomato paste and sugar.
8. Heat it for 6 min. Serve your soup hot with your favorite toppings.
9. Enjoy..

CARIBBEAN
Prawns

Prep Time: 20 mins
Total Time: 28 mins

Servings per Recipe: 8

Calories	264.5 kcal
Fat	15.4 g
Cholesterol	236.2 mg
Sodium	1068.0 mg
Carbohydrates	4.6 g
Protein	25.8 g

Ingredients

3 1/2 lb. raw prawns
Marinade
1/2 C. olive oil
1/3 C. lemon juice
1 onion, peeled and quartered
6 cloves garlic, peeled

5 cm ginger, peeled
1 tsp chili powder
salt and pepper

Directions

1. Place a large pan over medium heat. Heat in it the oil.
2. Get a blender: Combine in it all the marinade ingredients. Blend them smooth.
3. Get a mixing bowl: Stir in it the marinade with prawns. Let them sit for 2 h in the fridge.
4. Before you do anything else, preheat the grill and grease it.
5. Drain the prawns from the marinade and place them over the grill.
6. Put on the lid and let them cook for 10 to 14 min. Serve them hot.
7. Enjoy..

Brussels
Sprouts Mongolian

Prep Time: 15 mins
Total Time: 30 mins

Servings per Recipe: 8
Calories	56.0 kcal
Fat	2.6 g
Cholesterol	0.0 mg
Sodium	267.2 mg
Carbohydrates	7.1 g
Protein	2.5 g

Ingredients

2 (10 oz.) containers Brussels sprouts, trimmed and quartered
2 tbsp soy sauce
2 tsp fresh ginger, peeled & grated
1 tsp sesame oil
1 tbsp olive oil
1 large onion, halved & sliced
2 tbsp water

Directions

1. Get a mixing bowl: Whisk in it the soy sauce, grated ginger and sesame oil.
2. Place a large pan over medium heat. Heat in it the olive oil. Cook in it the onion for 6 min.
3. Turn the heat to high. Stir in the water with brussels sprouts. Put on the lid and let them cook for 6 min.
4. Remove the lid and let them cook for an extra 6 min. Turn off the heat and add the ginger mixture.
5. Stir them well. Serve your brussels sprouts right away with your favorite toppings.
6. Enjoy..

ASIAN
Fusion Cake

Prep Time: 20 mins
Total Time: 1 hr 35 mins

Servings per Recipe: 1
Calories	4248.2 kcal
Fat	206.2 g
Cholesterol	1232.0 mg
Sodium	5148.1 mg
Carbohydrates	544.0 g
Protein	59.3 g

Ingredients

1 C. butter
1 1/2 C. sugar
2 tsp vanilla extract
1/2 tsp almond extract
4 eggs
2 1/2 C. all-purpose flour

2 1/2 tsp baking powder
1 tsp salt
1 1/2 C. Greek yogurt
3/4 C. crystallized ginger, cut into pieces

Directions

1. Before you do anything, preheat the oven to 300 F.
2. Grease a cake pan with some butter and place it aside.
3. Get a mixing bowl: Cream in it the butter until it becomes light.
4. Mix in the sugar with vanilla and almond extract. Beat them until they become smooth.
5. Beat in the eggs gradually followed by flower, baking powder, yogurt and salt. Add the ginger and mix them well.
6. Pour the batter into the greased pan. Place it in the oven and let it cook for 76 min.
7. Allow the cake to cool down completely then serve it with your favorite toppings.
8. Enjoy..

My
First Chutney

🥣 Prep Time: 1 hr
🕐 Total Time: 2 hrs 30 mins

Servings per Recipe: 1
Calories	385.5 kcal
Fat	0.2 g
Cholesterol	0.0 mg
Sodium	200.4 mg
Carbohydrates	97.8 g
Protein	0.9 g

Ingredients

10 C. peeled chopped pears
4 C. granulated sugar
1 C. seedless raisin
1 C. chopped crystallized ginger
3 C. cider vinegar
1 tsp salt
1 tsp cinnamon

1/2 tsp ground allspice
1/2 tsp ground cloves

Directions

1. Place a large saucepan over medium heat. Stir in it all the ingredients.
2. Cook them until they start boiling while stirring them all the time.
3. Lower the heat and let them cook for 90 min uncovered.
4. Once the time is up, turn off the heat and transfer the chutney into mason jars.
5. Seal them and place them in a dark area until ready to serve.
6. Enjoy..

CHINESE
Buffet Beef

Prep Time: 20 mins
Total Time: 35 mins

Servings per Recipe: 3
Calories	424.2 kcal
Fat	22.0 g
Cholesterol	102.8 mg
Sodium	2861.4 mg
Carbohydrates	17.5 g
Protein	37.5 g

Ingredients

2 tbsp canola oil
1/2 tsp minced ginger
1/2 C. broccoli floret
1/2 C. carrot, slices
1/2 C. green beans, chopped
1/2 C. red onion, sliced

3/4 C. teriyaki sauce
1 lb. beef sirloin flank steak, sliced

Directions

1. Place a large pan over high heat. Heat in it the oil.
2. Cook in it the veggies with ginger for 6 min. Stir in the beef and cook them for 4 min.
3. Add the teriyaki sauce. Cook them for 2 min. Serve your stir fry hot.
4. Enjoy..

Leafy
Greens Lunch Box Salad with Ginger Vinaigrette

Prep Time: 20 mins
Total Time: 20 mins

Servings per Recipe: 4

Calories	136.2 kcal
Fat	10.6 g
Cholesterol	0.0 mg
Sodium	396.5 mg
Carbohydrates	8.8 g
Protein	3.1 g

Ingredients

3 tbsp minced onions
3 tbsp peanut oil
2 tbsp distilled white vinegar
1 1/2 tbsp grated ginger
1 tbsp ketchup
1 tbsp reduced sodium soy sauce
1/4 tsp minced garlic

1/4 tsp kosher sea salt
ground pepper
10 oz. spinach
1 large carrot, grated
1 medium red bell pepper, sliced

Directions

1. Get a food processor: Place in it the onion, oil, vinegar, ginger, ketchup, soy sauce, garlic, salt and pepper.
2. Blend them smooth.
3. Get a mixing bowl: Toss in it onion mixture with carrot, bell pepper and spinach.
4. Serve your salad right away.
5. Enjoy..

MALAYSIAN
Basmati

Prep Time: 5 mins
Total Time: 35 mins

Servings per Recipe: 6
Calories	210.5 kcal
Fat	1.4 g
Cholesterol	0.0 mg
Sodium	200.2 mg
Carbohydrates	45.5 g
Protein	3.7 g

Ingredients

2 C. apple juice
3/4 C. water
1/2 tsp salt
1 1/2 C. white basmati rice

2 slices ginger, slices
1 piece cinnamon stick

Directions

1. Place a large saucepan over medium heat. Stir in the water with salt.
2. Cook them until they start boiling. Lower the heat and stir in the rest of the ingredients.
3. Put on the lid and let them cook for 28 min. Drain and discard the ginger with cinnamon stick.
4. Fluff your rice with a fork then serve it.
5. Enjoy..

Tomato
Bisque

Prep Time: 5 mins
Total Time: 10 mins

Servings per Recipe: 4

Calories	213.9 kcal
Fat	18.5 g
Cholesterol	0.0 mg
Sodium	431.2 mg
Carbohydrates	12.8 g
Protein	2.9 g

Ingredients

1 (10 3/4 oz.) cans condensed tomato soup
1 1/2 C. canned unsweetened coconut milk

1 tbsp grated ginger

Directions

1. Place a heavy saucepan over medium heat. Combine in it the soup with coconut milk and ginger.
2. Cook them until they start boiling while always stirring.
3. Adjust the seasoning of your soup then serve it hot.
4. Enjoy..

CHEESECAKE
Shanghai

🥣 Prep Time: 20 mins
🕐 Total Time: 55 mins

Servings per Recipe: 12	
Calories	223.8 kcal
Fat	14.6 g
Cholesterol	56.6 mg
Sodium	68.1 mg
Carbohydrates	20.5 g
Protein	3.0 g

Ingredients

1 1/4 C. flour
1/3 C. sugar
1/2 C. sweet butter
2 tbsp candied orange peel, chopped
8 oz. cream cheese, softened
1/4 C. sugar

1 large egg
1 tbsp lemon juice
1/2 C. candied pineapple, chopped
1/8 C. candied ginger, chopped

Directions

1. Before you do anything, preheat the oven to 350 F.
2. To prepare the crumble:
3. Get a mixing bowl: Mix in it the flour, sugar, butter and candied orange peel.
4. Grease a baking pan. Spread in it half of the flour mixture. Place it in the oven and let it cook for 14 min.
5. Place it aside to cool down.
6. To prepare the filling:
7. Get a mixing bowl: Cream in it the cheese, sugar, egg and lemon juice until they become smooth.
8. Fold the ginger and candied pineapple into the batter. Pour it over the crust.
9. Sprinkle the remaining flour mixture over it.
10. Place the pan in the oven and let it cook for 18 min.
11. Place the pan aside to cool down completely. Cut it into squares then serve them.
12. Enjoy..

Vanilla
Crispies

Prep Time: 2 hrs 15 mins
Total Time: 2 hrs 30 mins

Servings per Recipe: 48

Calories	73.3 kcal
Fat	4.2 g
Cholesterol	12.0 mg
Sodium	33.4 mg
Carbohydrates	8.4 g
Protein	0.9 g

Ingredients

- 1 C. quick-cooking oatmeal, ground
- 3/4 C. pecan halves, ground
- 1 C. whole wheat flour
- 1/4 C. cornstarch
- 1 tsp ground ginger
- 1/2 tsp salt
- 1/4 tsp baking soda
- 3/4 C. unsalted butter, softened
- 3/4 C. granulated sugar
- 1/3 C. light brown sugar
- 1 tsp pure vanilla extract
- 1 large egg

Directions

1. Before you do anything, preheat the oven to 350 F.
2. Lined up a baking pan with wax sheet and place it aside.
3. Get a food processor: Place in it the pecan pieces with oatmeal.
4. Pulse them several times until they become finely chopped.
5. Get a large mixing bowl: Stir in it the wheat flour, cornstarch, ginger, salt and baking soda.
6. Get a mixing bowl: Cream in it the butter until it becomes light and fluffy.
7. Mix in the granulated and light brown sugar until they become smooth.
8. Beat in the egg and vanilla extract. Add the flour mixture gradually while mixing them until you get a soft dough.
9. Press the dough into the pan in an even layer. Place it in the fridge and let it sit for 120 min.
10. Cut the dough into small bars.
11. Place it in the oven and let it cook for 17 to 19 min.
12. Allow the cookies to cool down completely. Serve them with some tea.
13. Enjoy..

ASIAN
Cabbage Stir Fry

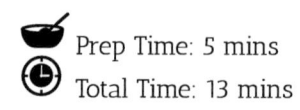 Prep Time: 5 mins
Total Time: 13 mins

Servings per Recipe: 4
Calories	71.0 kcal
Fat	6.8 g
Cholesterol	0.0 mg
Sodium	1.2 mg
Carbohydrates	2.6 g
Protein	0.3 g

Ingredients

1 head savoy cabbage, cored, shredded
2 tbsp lite olive oil
1 tbsp minced garlic
salt & pepper

1 1/4 tbsp ginger, minced
1 lime, juice

Directions

1. Place a large pan over high heat. Heat in it the oil.
2. Cook in it the cabbage for 3 min. Stir in the garlic with salt and pepper.
3. Cook them for one minute. Stir in the ginger and cook them for another minute.
4. Turn off the heat and stir in the lime juice. Serve your stir fried cabbage warm.
5. Enjoy..

Window Sill Tea Bread

Prep Time: 10 mins
Total Time: 55 mins

Servings per Recipe: 1
Calories	2764.7 kcal
Fat	100.3 g
Cholesterol	389.0 mg
Sodium	1833.7 mg
Carbohydrates	423.6 g
Protein	52.8 g

Ingredients

1 C. sugar
1/2 C. margarine
2 eggs
2 C. flour
3 tsp baking powder
1 tsp ground ginger
1/2 C. orange juice

1/2 C. milk
1 tsp orange rind, grated
1/2 C. walnuts, chopped

Directions

1. Before you do anything, preheat the oven to 356 F.
2. Get a mixing bowl: Beat in it the sugar with margarine until they become light and fluffy.
3. Mix in the eggs gradually until they become smooth. Add the flour with ginger, and a pinch of salt. Mix them well.
4. Stir the orange zest and walnuts into the mixture.
5. Pour the mixture into a greased loaf pan. Place it in the oven and let it cook for 46 min.
6. Enjoy.

RISING
Sun Soup

🍲 Prep Time: 30 mins
🕐 Total Time: 1 hr 35 mins

Servings per Recipe: 6
Calories	75.3 kcal
Fat	2.6 g
Cholesterol	0.0 mg
Sodium	370.5 mg
Carbohydrates	12.6 g
Protein	1.4 g

Ingredients

3 medium beets, peeled and cut into chunks
1 C. onion
1 tbsp canola oil
1 lb. carrot
1 large garlic clove
1 tbsp minced ginger

6 C. water
1 tsp grated orange peel
3/4 tsp salt
pepper
4 tsp sour cream

Directions

1. Place a large saucepan over medium heat. Heat in it the oil. Cook in it the onion for 4 min.
2. Stir in the carrot and cook them for 9 min. Stir in the ginger, garlic, and orange peel.
3. Cook them for 1 min. Stir in the stock and bring them to a boil. Lower the heat and put on the lid.
4. Let them cook for 52 min until the veggies become soft.
5. Turn off the heat and allow the soup to cool down completely.
6. Transfer it to a blender and blend them smooth. Pour the soup back into the saucepan.
7. Heat the soup for few minutes then serve it hot.
8. Enjoy..

Chinese
Carrot Wok

🥘 Prep Time: 10 mins
🕐 Total Time: 18 mins

Servings per Recipe: 3
Calories	56.2 kcal
Fat	2.2 g
Cholesterol	0.0 mg
Sodium	59.2 mg
Carbohydrates	8.9 g
Protein	1.0 g

Ingredients

1 tsp sesame oil
2 C. carrots, sliced
1 1/2 tsp ginger, grated
1 tsp sesame seeds, toasted and chopped

1 clove garlic, chopped
salt

Directions

1. Place a large pan over medium heat. Heat in it the oil.
2. Cook in it the carrots, garlic and ginger for 6 min.
3. Stir in the sesame seeds. Put on the lid and let them coo for 4 min.
4. Serve your fried carrots warm.
5. Enjoy..

SWEET
Shibuya Salsa

Prep Time: 10 mins
Total Time: 10 mins

Servings per Recipe: 1
Calories   209.7 kcal
Fat   13.7 g
Cholesterol   0.0 mg
Sodium   512.3 mg
Carbohydrates   22.6 g
Protein   2.7 g

Ingredients

1/2 cucumber, peeled, de-seeded and diced
1 tbsp fresh ginger, grated
1/2 lemon, juice
1 tbsp extra virgin olive oil
1/2 tbsp soy sauce
1/2 tsp wasabi paste, see note

2 tsp honey, slightly softened
2 green onions, green and white parts, sliced
1/2 C. Greek yogurt
Toppings
green onion, slices
black sesame seed

Directions

1. Place a large pan over medium heat. Heat in it the oil.
2. Get a mixing bowl: Combine in it all the ingredients. Season them with a pinch of salt and pepper.
3. Place your salsa in the fridge until ready to serve.
4. Enjoy.

NOTE: To make wasabi paste combine 3 tsps of store bought wasabi powder with 1 tsp of water. Stir the mix until it is smooth, add more water if needed.

Grilled
Ginger Tilapia

🥣 Prep Time: 35 mins
🕐 Total Time: 50 mins

Servings per Recipe: 4
Calories	230.6 kcal
Fat	3.2 g
Cholesterol	85.1 mg
Sodium	1600.9 mg
Carbohydrates	13.0 g
Protein	38.3 g

Ingredients

1 1/2 lbs. tilapia fillets
6 tbsp soy sauce
2 tbsp apple cider vinegar
1 tbsp orange zest
1/4 C. orange juice
2 tbsp ginger, grated
3 tbsp garlic, chopped

3 scallions, chopped
3/4 C. orange juice

Directions

1. Reserve 3/4 C. of orange juice.
2. Season the tilapia fillets with some salt and pepper.
3. Get a mixing bowl: Mix in it the remaining ingredients to make the marinade.
4. Add to it the fish fillet and cover it. Let them sit for 12 min.
5. Before you do anything, preheat the grill and grease it.
6. Drain the fish fillets and place the marinade aside.
7. Lay o it the fish fillets and cook them for 2 to 4 min on each side.
8. Place a heavy saucepan over medium heat. Stir in it the marinade with the reserved orange juice.
9. Cook them until they start boiling. Lower the heat and let it cook until it reduces by two thirds.
10. Drizzle the sauce over your fish fillets then serve them warm.
11. Enjoy..

MONGOLIAN
Green Beans

Prep Time: 10 mins
Total Time: 25 mins

Servings per Recipe: 10

Calories	86.9 kcal
Fat	5.6 g
Cholesterol	0.0 mg
Sodium	22.8 mg
Carbohydrates	8.9 g
Protein	2.1 g

Ingredients

1 pinch salt
2 1/2 lbs. string beans, trimmed
4 tbsp vegetable oil
1/4 C. minced ginger, peeled

4 medium garlic cloves, minced

Directions

1. Place a large pot of salted water over medium heat. Cook in it half of the green beans for 6 min.
2. Drain them and place them in an icy bowl of water. Drain them again and place them aside.
3. Repeat the process with the other half.
4. Place a pan over high heat. Heat in it 2 tbsp of oil.
5. Cook in it half of the green beans with half of the garlic, ginger, a pinch of salt and pepper for 2 min.
6. Transfer the mixture to a serving plate. Repeat the process with the remaining beans. Serve them warm.
7. Enjoy..

Teriyaki
Fish

Prep Time: 35 mins
Total Time: 45 mins

Servings per Recipe: 2
Calories	258.5 kcal
Fat	10.9 g
Cholesterol	59.0 mg
Sodium	2831.5 mg
Carbohydrates	13.2 g
Protein	25.1 g

Ingredients

- 1/3 C. soy sauce
- 2 tbsp white vinegar
- 2 1/2 tbsp cider vinegar
- 1 - 2 tbsp honey
- 1 1/2 tbsp peeled chopped gingerroot
- 2 salmon steaks
- butter
- salt and pepper

Directions

1. Place a saucepan over medium heat. Stir all the sauce ingredients. Let them cook until it reduces by half.
2. Turn off the heat and let the sauce cool completely.
3. Before you do anything else, preheat the oven broiler.
4. Line up a pan with a piece of foil. Place in it the fish fillets.
5. Coat it with melted butter then season it with a pinch of salt and pepper.
6. Cook it in the oven for 4 to 6 min. Drizzle the sauce over the fish fillets then serve them hot.
7. Enjoy..

THAI
Peanut Penne

Prep Time: 20 mins
Total Time: 30 mins

Servings per Recipe: 4
Calories	762.5 kcal
Fat	21.0 g
Cholesterol	71.6 mg
Sodium	432.4 mg
Carbohydrates	110.8 g
Protein	37.4 g

Ingredients

1 lb. penne pasta
3 boneless chicken breasts, skinned and chopped
1 tbsp cornstarch
2/3 C. low-fat milk
1/4 C. creamy peanut butter
2 limes, juice
2 tbsp reduced sodium soy sauce

2 tbsp honey
2 garlic cloves, chopped
1 tsp ginger, grated
3 tbsp cilantro, chopped
4 tsp crushed red pepper flakes
1/4 C. chopped chives

Directions

1. Prepare the pasta by following the instructions on the package.
2. Place a large pan over medium heat. Coat it with a cooking spray.
3. Cook in it the chicken breasts for 3 to 4 min on each side. Place it aside.
4. Get a mixing bowl: Mix in it the cornstarch with 2 tbsp of milk.
5. Stir the mixture into to it the rest of the milk and cook them for 1 min.
6. Lower the heat and let them cook for 2 min.
7. Get a mixing bowl: Whisk in it the peanut butter, lime juice, soy sauce, honey, garlic, ginger, and red pepper.
8. Add the mixture to the pan and stir them well. Turn off the heat.
9. Place the pasta on serving plates. Top it with the chicken breasts and drizzle the sauce over them.
10. Serve them right away.
11. Enjoy..

Lemon
Chicken BBQ

Prep Time: 2 hrs
Total Time: 2 hrs

Servings per Recipe: 3
Calories	338.2 kcal
Fat	14.4 g
Cholesterol	128.6 mg
Sodium	694.3 mg
Carbohydrates	2.1 g
Protein	47.2 g

Ingredients

1 tsp black pepper
3/4 tsp salt
3/4 tsp ginger
3 medium garlic cloves, crushed

2 tbsp olive oil
1 tbsp lemon juice
1 - 1 1/2 lb. skinless chicken

Directions

1. Get a mixing bowl: Stir in it the salt, ginger, pepper, garlic, oil, and lemon juice.
2. Use a skewer to pierce the chicken several times. Coat them with the ginger mix. Let them sit for 120 min.
3. Before you do anything, preheat the grill and grease it.
4. Place over it the chicken and let it cook until it is done to your liking.
5. Enjoy..

GINGER
Broccoli Stir Fry

🥣 Prep Time: 5 mins
🕐 Total Time: 10 mins

Servings per Recipe: 4
Calories	63.5 kcal
Fat	3.8 g
Cholesterol	0.0 mg
Sodium	222.3 mg
Carbohydrates	6.1 g
Protein	2.7 g

Ingredients

12 oz. Chinese broccoli, cut into pieces
1/4 C. homemade chicken broth
1 1/2 tsp shao hosing apple cider
1 tsp ginger juice
1/2 tsp cornstarch
1/4 tsp salt

1/8 tsp sugar
1 tbsp vegetable oil
3 slices ginger

Directions

1. Get a mixing bowl: Whisk in it the broth, apple cider, ginger juice, cornstarch, salt, and sugar.
2. Place a large pan over high heat. Heat in it the oil. Heat in it the oil.
3. Cook in it the ginger for 12 sec. Stir in the broccoli and cook them for 2 min.
4. Add the broth and cook them for 1 min. Serve your stir fry hot with some rice.
5. Enjoy..

Glazed
Baby Carrots

🥣 Prep Time: 5 mins
🕐 Total Time: 20 mins

Servings per Recipe: 6
Calories	127.2 kcal
Fat	8.0 g
Cholesterol	20.3 mg
Sodium	240.4 mg
Carbohydrates	13.2 g
Protein	1.4 g

Ingredients

1 1/2 lbs. baby carrots, cut into diagonal slices
3/4 C. chicken broth
4 tbsp butter
1 1/2 tbsp brown sugar

2 tbsp grated ginger
1 tbsp chopped parsley

Directions

1. Place a large saucepan over medium heat. Stir in it the carrots, broth, butter, brown sugar, and ginger.
2. Put on the lid and let them cook for 11 min. Remove the cover and let them cook for 6 min.
3. Stir in the parsley. Serve your glazed carrots warm.
4. Enjoy..

CHICKEN
Cutlet with Ginger Aioli

Prep Time: 15 mins
Total Time: 25 mins

Servings per Recipe: 4
Calories	214.7 kcal
Fat	9.6 g
Cholesterol	80.6 mg
Sodium	276.8 mg
Carbohydrates	5.8 g
Protein	25.3 g

Ingredients

4 boneless skinless chicken breasts, halved
1 - 2 tsp Cajun seasoning, see appendix
1/3 C. mayonnaise
1 tbsp ginger, minced
1 lime, juice

1 dash Tabasco sauce
salt and pepper

Directions

1. Before you do anything, preheat the grill and grease it.
2. Place the chicken breasts halves between two sheets. lb. them until they become flat.
3. Get a mixing bowl: Whisk in it the mayonnaise, ginger, lime juice, tabasco and salt and pepper.
4. Coat the chicken breasts with the mixture. Sprinkle over them the Cajun seasoning.
5. Place them on the grill and let them cook for 5 to 7 min on each side.
6. Serve your grilled chicken warm.
7. Enjoy..

April
Pecan Pie

Prep Time: 30 mins
Total Time: 1 hr 20 mins

Servings per Recipe: 8

Calories	384.5 kcal
Fat	28.3 g
Cholesterol	107.9 mg
Sodium	126.1 mg
Carbohydrates	29.5 g
Protein	4.6 g

Ingredients

Crust
1/2 C. unsalted butter
1/3 C. cream cheese
1 C. all-purpose flour
Insides
1/3 C. unsalted butter, melted
1/2 C. Splenda brown sugar blend
2 large eggs

1 tbsp grated ginger
1/2 tsp ground cinnamon
1/2 tsp vanilla extract
1/4 tsp salt
2 C. peeled and sliced baking apples
1/2 C. pecan halves

Directions

1. To prepare the crust:
2. Get a mixing bowl: Cream in it the cream cheese with butter. Mix in the flour with a pinch of salt.
3. Place the dough in a greased bowl and cover it. Let it rest in the fridge for 120 min.
4. Before you do anything else, preheat the oven to 375 F.
5. Place the dough on a floured surface. Flatten it into a 1/4 inch thick disk.
6. Place it in a greased pie pan. Cook it in the oven for 8 min. Place it aside to cool down completely.
7. To prepare the filling:
8. Get a large mixing bowl: Cream in it the Splenda with butter.
9. Add the eggs gradually while mixing them at the same time. Mix in the ginger, cinnamon, vanilla and salt.
10. Lay the apple slices and pecans in the pie shell. Pour the filling over them.
11. Place the pie in the oven and let it cook for 45 to 52 min.
12. Allow the pie to cool down completely. Serve it with your favorite toppings.
13. Enjoy..

INDONESIAN
Penne

Prep Time: 25 mins
Total Time: 1 hr 5 mins

Servings per Recipe: 4
Calories	568.1 kcal
Fat	26.3 g
Cholesterol	40.8 mg
Sodium	862.8 mg
Carbohydrates	63.4 g
Protein	18.9 g

Ingredients

2 tbsp butter
1 C. chopped onion
1 large granny smith apple, peeled and cored, and cut into pieces
3 cloves garlic, minced
2 tsp curry powder
1/2 C. dry marsala
1 C. chicken stock
2 tsp fish sauce

1 tsp Thai red curry paste, see appendix
1 1/2 C. canned unsweetened coconut milk
1/2 lb. penne pasta
1/2 lb. crabmeat, flaked
3 tbsp chopped basil
ginger based chutney, see appendix

Directions

1. Place a large pan over medium heat. Heat in it the butter. Cook in it the onion with apple and garlic for 7 min.
2. Add the curry powder with marsala. Cook them until they start boiling.
3. Lower the heat and let them cook for 2 to 3 min.
4. Stir in the stock, fish sauce, and curry paste. Cook them for 6 min.
5. Stir in the coconut milk and cook them for 4 min. Add the crabmeat with a pinch of salt and pepper.
6. Prepare the pasta by following the instructions on the package. Drain it.
7. Stir the pasta into the sauce and heat them for 2 to 3 min. Serve it hot.
8. Enjoy.

Orange
Asparagus

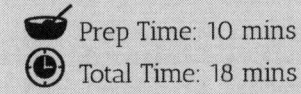

Prep Time: 10 mins
Total Time: 18 mins

Servings per Recipe: 4
Calories	60.4 kcal
Fat	1.8 g
Cholesterol	0.0 mg
Sodium	2.7 mg
Carbohydrates	9.4 g
Protein	3.4 g

Ingredients

1 lb. fresh asparagus, trimmed
1/2 C. orange juice
1 tsp orange zest, grated
1 1/2 tsp cornstarch

1 inch gingerroot, peeled and grated
2 tbsp slivered almonds, toasted

Directions

1. Put the asparagus spears in a steamer. Cook them for 6 min.
2. Place a heavy saucepan over medium heat. Combine in it the juice, zest and cornstarch.
3. Bring them to a boil. Lower the heat and let the sauce cook for 4 min.
4. Turn off the heat and stir in the ginger.
5. Transfer the asparagus on a serving plate. Drizzle over them the orange sauce.
6. Serve them right away.
7. Enjoy.

HOW
to Make Squid

Prep Time: 5 mins
Total Time: 30 mins

Servings per Recipe: 2
Calories	391.6 kcal
Fat	17.3 g
Cholesterol	583.5 mg
Sodium	1711.8 mg
Carbohydrates	13.8 g
Protein	42.4 g

Ingredients

17.5 oz. squid, sliced
2 tbsp ginger, grated
3 tbsp soy sauce

2 tbsp white vinegar
2 tbsp vegetable oil

Directions

1. Get a mixing bowl: Mix in it the ginger with white vinegar and soy sauce. Stir in the squid slices.
2. Let it sit for 20 min.
3. Place a large pan over high heat. Heat in it the oil.
4. Drain the squid slices and add them to the pan. Stir fry them for 7 to 8 min.
5. Add the rest of the marinade and cook them for 2 min.
6. Serve your stir fried squid with some rice and veggies.
7. Enjoy..

Cucumber
Salsa

🥣 Prep Time: 15 mins
🕐 Total Time: 4 hrs 15 mins

Servings per Recipe: 1	
Calories	221.5 kcal
Fat	0.1 g
Cholesterol	0.0 mg
Sodium	4.3 mg
Carbohydrates	55.3 g
Protein	0.8 g

Ingredients

1/3 C. water
1 C. sugar
1/2 C. vinegar
1 cucumber, sliced

1 tsp ginger
1 yellow onion, chopped

Directions

1. Place a large pan over medium heat. Heat in it the oil.
2. Get a mixing bowl: Whisk in it the water, vinegar and sugar.
3. Stir in the cucumber, ginger and onion.
4. Place the salsa in the fridge for an overnight then serve it.
5. Enjoy..

MID-OCTOBER
Muffins

Prep Time: 12 mins
Total Time: 35 mins

Servings per Recipe: 12
Calories	152.1 kcal
Fat	7.6 g
Cholesterol	25.9 mg
Sodium	146.0 mg
Carbohydrates	19.1 g
Protein	2.7 g

Ingredients

nonstick cooking spray
1/4 C. unsalted butter
1/2 C. brown sugar
1 large egg
1/2 C. canned pumpkin puree
1 tsp grated gingerroot
1 C. all-purpose flour
1/4 tsp baking soda
1 tsp baking powder

1/4 tsp salt
1 pinch black pepper
1/4 tsp ground cinnamon
1/4 tsp ground cloves
1/4 tsp ground allspice
1/3 C. low-fat buttermilk
1/2 C. minced crystallized ginger
1/2 C. minced walnuts

Directions

1. Before you do anything, preheat the oven to 350 F.
2. Grease a 12 C. muffin pan with a cooking spray.
3. Get a mixing bowl: Cream in it the butter with sugar until they become light and smooth.
4. Mix in the eggs followed by pumpkin purée and ginger.
5. Get a mixing bowl: Stir in it the flour, baking soda, baking powder, salt, cinnamon, cloves and allspice.
6. Add them gradually to the butter mixture while mixing all the time until they become smooth.
7. Fold the crystallized ginger into the batter. Pour it into the muffin pan.
8. Sprinkle over them the chopped nuts. Place the muffin pan in the oven and let them cook for 26 min.
9. Allow the muffins to cool down completely. Serve them with your favorite toppings.
10. Enjoy..

Rhubarb
Squares

Prep Time: 25 mins
Total Time: 1 hr 20 mins

Servings per Recipe: 16
Calories   214.0 kcal
Fat   9.2 g
Cholesterol   22.8 mg
Sodium   66.4 mg
Carbohydrates   31.3 g
Protein   2.3 g

Ingredients

1 1/2 C. quick-cooking oats
1 C. all-purpose flour
3/4 C. brown sugar
3/4 C. butter
1/4 C. granulated sugar
2 tbsp all-purpose flour
1/2 tsp ground ginger

2 C. sliced rhubarb
Icing
3/4 C. powdered sugar, sifted
1/4 tsp ground ginger
3 - 4 tsp orange juice

Directions

1. Before you do anything, preheat the oven to 350 F.
2. Cover a baking pan with a piece of foil.
3. Place a large pan over medium heat. Heat in it the oil.
4. Get a mixing bowl: Mix in it the oats, 1 C. flour, and brown sugar. Add the butter and mix them well.
5. Reserve 1 C. of the crumble mixture. Pour the remaining mixture into the lined up pan.
6. Cook it in the oven for 26 min to make the crust.
7. Get a mixing bowl: Mix in it the granulated sugar, 2 Tbsp flour, and ground ginger.
8. Add the rhubarb and stir them well. Spread the mixture over the crust.
9. Top it with the reserved C. of crumble. Place it in the oven and cook it for 32 to 36 min.
10. Once the time is up, place the pan aside and let it cool down completely.
11. Get a mixing bowl: Whisk in it the powdered sugar, ground ginger, and orange juice.
12. Drizzle the icing over the rhubarb pan. Slice it into bars then serve it.
13. Enjoy..

BACKYARD
Thai Shrimp

Prep Time: 10 mins
Total Time: 30 mins

Servings per Recipe: 4
Calories	143.1 kcal
Fat	2.6 g
Cholesterol	220.8 mg
Sodium	264.8 mg
Carbohydrates	4.0 g
Protein	25.5 g

Ingredients

1 lb. medium raw shrimp, peeled and
deveined
1 C. sliced mushroom
2 C. broccoli florets
1 small red bell pepper, strips
2 cloves garlic, minced

1/2 tsp grated, minced ginger
1 tsp dark sesame oil

Directions

1. Before you do anything, preheat the grill and grease it.
2. Get a large piece of foil. Place in it the shrimp with veggies, ginger, garlic and oil.
3. Sprinkle over them some salt and pepper. Pull the foil sides on top and crunch it to seal it.
4. Place the foil packet over the grill. Let it cook for 16 to 22 min.
5. Serve your grilled shrimp and veggies packet hot.
6. Enjoy..

Roasted
Honey Kale Bites

🥣 Prep Time: 15 mins
🕐 Total Time: 4 hrs 15 mins

Servings per Recipe: 4
Calories   98.8 kcal
Fat   5.7 g
Cholesterol   0.0 mg
Sodium   273.2 mg
Carbohydrates   10.1 g
Protein   4.2 g

Ingredients

1 bunch kale
1/4 C. unsalted almonds
1 tbsp lemon juice
2 tsp honey
1 tbsp tamari

1 inch ginger, grated
1 dash cayenne

Directions

1. Get a blender: Place in it the almonds with lemon juice, honey, tamari, ginger and cayenne. Blend them smooth.
2. Add water if needed to make the marinade.
3. Coat the kale leaves with the mixture. Place them on a baking sheet.
4. Place it oven and heat it on the lowest temperature. For 130 F Let them cook for 4 to 6 h until they become dry and crunchy.
5. Allow the kale chips to cool down completely then serve them.
6. Enjoy..

JAKARTA
Quinoa Bowls

Prep Time: 15 mins
Total Time: 15 mins

Servings per Recipe: 4
Calories	342.7 kcal
Fat	18.9 g
Cholesterol	22.9 mg
Sodium	124.2 mg
Carbohydrates	34.9 g
Protein	9.6 g

Ingredients

Vinaigrette
2 tbsp lime juice, squeezed
1 tbsp seasoned apple cider vinegar
1 tsp ginger, minced
1 small garlic clove, minced
salt
1 pinch cayenne
2 tsp sesame oil
1/4 C. canola oil
2 tbsp buttermilk

Quinoa
3 C. cooked quinoa
4 scallions, white and light green parts, sliced
1 small cucumber, halved, seeded and sliced diagonally
1/4 C. chopped cilantro
12 -16 cooked medium shrimp, peeled

Directions

1. Place a large pan over medium heat. Heat in it the oil.
2. Get a mixing bowl: Mix in it the lime juice, apple cider vinegar, ginger, garlic, salt, cayenne, sesame oil, canola oil, and buttermilk.
3. Get a large serving bowl: Place in it the quinoa, scallions, cucumber, and cilantro.
4. Drizzle the dressing on top. Mix the salad well. Garnish it with shrimp then serve it right away.
5. Enjoy..

Bronzed
Yams with Scallops

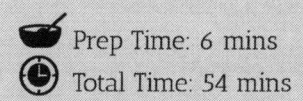 Prep Time: 6 mins
Total Time: 54 mins

Servings per Recipe: 1	
Calories	211.2 kcal
Fat	3.4 g
Cholesterol	28.6 mg
Sodium	715.1 mg
Carbohydrates	31.2 g
Protein	13.6 g

Ingredients

Yams
4 medium sweet potatoes, scrubbed
1/2 C. skim milk
1 inch gingerroot, peeled and grated
1/2 tsp salt
1/4 tsp ground pepper

Scallops
1 tbsp unsalted butter
3/4 lb. large scallop, sliced in rounds
2 scallions, sliced

Directions

1. Before you do anything, preheat the oven to 400 F.
2. Use a fork or skewer to poke several holes in the potatoes.
3. Place them on a baking tray. Cook them in the oven for 46 min.
4. Once the time is up, place the potatoes aside to cool down for a while. Peel them.
5. Get a mixing bowl: Combine in it the potato with milk, ginger, salt and pepper. Beat them until they become creamy.
6. Place a pan over high heat. Heat in it the butter.
7. Cook in it the scallops for 1 to 2 min on each side while spooning over them the melted butter.
8. Serve your golden scallops with the mashed sweet potato.
9. Enjoy..

BRONZED
Yams with Scallops

🥘 Prep Time: 6 mins
🕐 Total Time: 54 mins

Servings per Recipe: 4
Calories	211.2 kcal
Fat	3.4 g
Cholesterol	28.6 mg
Sodium	715.1 mg
Carbohydrates	31.2 g
Protein	13.6 g

Ingredients

Yams
4 medium sweet potatoes, scrubbed
1/2 C. skim milk
1 inch gingerroot, peeled and grated
1/2 tsp salt
1/4 tsp ground pepper

Scallops
1 tbsp unsalted butter
3/4 lb. large scallop, sliced in rounds
2 scallions, sliced

Directions

1. Before you do anything, preheat the oven to 400 F.
2. Use a fork or skewer to poke several holes in the potatoes.
3. Place them on a baking tray. Cook them in the oven for 46 min.
4. Once the time is up, place the potatoes aside to cool down for a while. Peel them.
5. Get a mixing bowl: Combine in it the potato with milk, ginger, salt and pepper. Beat them until they become creamy.
6. Place a pan over high heat. Heat in it the butter.
7. Cook in it the scallops for 1 to 2 min on each side while spooning over them the melted butter.
8. Serve your golden scallops with the mashed sweet potato.
9. Enjoy..

Glazed
Ginger Chicken

Prep Time: 10 mins
Total Time: 24 mins

Servings per Recipe: 4

Calories	395.5 kcal
Fat	25.6 g
Cholesterol	127.5 mg
Sodium	649.5 mg
Carbohydrates	7.2 g
Protein	32.0 g

Ingredients

1 1/2 lbs. chicken, any part, chopped into pieces
2 tbsp ginger, peeled and chopped
2 tbsp sugar
1/2 tsp black pepper

1 1/2 tbsp fish sauce
1 tbsp scallion, chopped into pieces

Directions

1. Place a saucepan over high heat. Stir in it the sugar until it melts for 1 min.
2. Cook in it the ginger for 12 sec. Add the chicken with fish sauce, salt and pepper.
3. Cook them for 2 to 3 min. Lower the heat and let them cook until the sauce reduces by half and the chicken is done.
4. Serve your saucy chicken hot with some rice
5. Enjoy..

MOROCCAN
Apricots Chicken Tagine

🥣 Prep Time: 20 mins
🕐 Total Time: 55 mins

Servings per Recipe: 4
Calories	347.3 kcal
Fat	13.0 g
Cholesterol	80.2 mg
Sodium	168.8 mg
Carbohydrates	33.2 g
Protein	26.7 g

Ingredients

2 tbsp extra virgin olive oil
1 tbsp butter
1 onion, chopped
3 sprigs rosemary, 1 chopped, the other
2 cut halved
3 tbsp fresh ginger, peeled and chopped
2 red chilies, seeded and chopped
2 cinnamon sticks
1 lb. boneless skinless chicken breast

3/4 C. dried apricot
2 tbsp honey
1 (14 oz.) cans plum tomatoes, with their juice
sea salt
ground black pepper
4 tbsp basil, shredded

Directions

1. Place a tagine or stew pot over medium heat. Heat in it the butter with oil.
2. Cook in it the ginger, onion, chopped rosemary, and chilies for 3 min.
3. add the cinnamon sticks with rosemary sprigs and chicken. Cook them for 4 min.
4. Stir in the honey with apricots, tomatoes and a splash of water.
5. Put on the lid and let them cook until they start boiling.
6. Lower the heat and let the stew cook for 38 to 42 min.
7. Serve your chicken tagine hot with some bread and toasted almonds.
8. Enjoy..

Oriental
House Glazed Fish

🥣 Prep Time: 10 mins
🕐 Total Time: 30 mins

Servings per Recipe: 1	
Calories	155.5 kcal
Fat	1.2 g
Cholesterol	73.7mg
Sodium	599.3 mg
Carbohydrates	2.6 g
Protein	31.9 g

Ingredients

3 tbsp rice vinegar
2 tbsp soy sauce
2 tbsp ginger, finely grated
4 (6 - 8 oz.) cod fish fillets, skinless
coarse salt

ground pepper
6 scallions, green tops only

Directions

1. Place a large pan over medium heat. Stir in it the vinegar, soy sauce, and ginger. Cook them for 1 min.
2. Sprinkle some salt and pepper over the cod fillets. Place them over the sauce.
3. Cook them until they start boiling. Lower the heat and put on the lid.
4. Let them cook for 7 to 8 min. Stir in the scallions and put on the lid.
5. Cook them for an extra 2 min. Serve your cod skillet hot.
6. Enjoy..

JAPANESE
Noodle Bowls

Prep Time: 15 mins
Total Time: 25 mins

Servings per Recipe: 3
Calories	402.0 kcal
Fat	10.9 g
Cholesterol	0.0 mg
Sodium	543.1 mg
Carbohydrates	70.6 g
Protein	4.2 g

Ingredients

8 oz. uncooked rice noodles
hot water
2 - 3 tbsp vegetable oil
1 tbsp gingerroot, grated
3 cloves garlic, minced
3 scallions, thinly
1 green chile, seeded and chopped

1/2 C. shredded carrot
20 snow peas, trimmed
1/2 tsp salt
1 dash sesame oil
1 dash hot chili oil
chopped cilantro leaves

Directions

1. Prepare the noodles by following the instructions on the package. Drain it.
2. Place a large pan over high heat. Heat in it the oil. Cook in it the garlic with ginger for 2 min.
3. Stir in the scallions, chili, carrots and snow peas. Cook them for 3 min.
4. Stir in the noodles with a pinch of salt. Heat for 2 min.
5. Add the sesame oil with chili oil. Turn of the heat. Serve your noodles hot.
6. Enjoy..

Asian-Fusion
Cauliflower

🥣 Prep Time: 10 mins
🕐 Total Time: 20 mins

Servings per Recipe: 4

Calories	136.0 kcal
Fat	10.8 g
Cholesterol	0.0 mg
Sodium	43.4 mg
Carbohydrates	8.7 g
Protein	3.3 g

Ingredients

3 tbsp vegetable oil
2 tsp yellow mustard seeds
2 tsp grated peeled gingerroot
1/2 tsp turmeric
1 head cauliflower, cut into florets

1 1/2 tsp lemon juice
3 tbsp chopped coriander

Directions

1. Place a large pan over medium heat. Heat in it the oil.
2. Sauté in it the mustard seeds with the lid on until they start popping.
3. Turn off the heat and stir in the ginger with turmeric. Cook them for 40 sec.
4. Stir in the cauliflower with 1/2 C. of water. Put on the lid and let them cook for 7 to 9 min.
5. Stir in the lemon juice with coriander, a pinch of salt and pepper.
6. Serve your stir fried cauliflower right away.
7. Enjoy..

TOPPED
Tokyo Fried Chicken

Prep Time: 45 mins
Total Time: 1 hr 15 mins

Servings per Recipe: 4	
Calories	333.5 kcal
Fat	21.1 g
Cholesterol	123.4 mg
Sodium	825.0 mg
Carbohydrates	12.1 g
Protein	22.4 g

Ingredients

4 chicken legs
1/2 tsp salt
Marinade
1 egg, lightly beaten
1/2 tsp salt
black pepper
3 tbsp sesame oil
3 - 4 tbsp flour
3 - 4 tbsp cornstarch
oil
Sauce

1 tbsp rice vinegar
1 tbsp Chinese black vinegar
2 tbsp sugar
2 tbsp soy sauce
2 tbsp water
Relish
6 tbsp minced green onions
2 tbsp minced ginger
2 tbsp minced parsley

Directions

1. Get a mixing bowl: Mix in it all the marinade ingredients.
2. Get a large zip lock bag. Place in it the chicken and pour the marinade over it.
3. Seal the bag and let it sit for 40 min.
4. To prepare the sauce:
5. Get a mixing bowl: Whisk in it all the sauce ingredients. Place it in the fridge.
6. To prepare the relish:
7. Get a mixing bowl: Mix in it all the relish ingredients. Place it in the fridge.
8. Place a large pot over high heat. Heat it in about 2 inches of oil.
9. Place in it the chicken pieces gently and cook them for 35 to 45 min until they become golden brown.
10. Drain the chicken pieces and place them on paper towels.
11. Serve your fried chicken with the vinegar sauce and relish. Enjoy..

Chinese
White Fish Skillet

Prep Time: 5 mins
Total Time: 15 mins

Servings per Recipe: 4

Calories	261.3 kcal
Fat	8.1 g
Cholesterol	114.8 mg
Sodium	944.1 mg
Carbohydrates	12.6 g
Protein	33.3 g

Ingredients

2 tsp sesame oil
1 tbsp peanut oil
2 tbsp shredded ginger
2 red chilies, shredded
1/3 C. reduced-sodium soy sauce
1/3 C. fish broth
2 tbsp brown sugar

4 (6 oz.) white fish fillets

Directions

1. Place a large pan over high heat. Heat in it the sesame and peanut oil.
2. Cook in it the chilies with ginger for 1 to 2 min. Stir in the soy sauce with sugar and broth.
3. Cook them for 1 min. Stir in the fish and let them cook for 3 to 4 min on each side.
4. Serve your glazed fish fillets hot with some rice.
5. Enjoy

4-INGREDIENT
Braised Lamb

Prep Time: 5 mins
Total Time: 11 mins

Servings per Recipe: 4
Calories	1038.9 kcal
Fat	75.9 g
Cholesterol	210.9 mg
Sodium	168.8 mg
Carbohydrates	5.0 g
Protein	46.6 g

Ingredients

6 lamb loin chops
salt and pepper
5 tbsp white grape juice

4 tbsp ginger marmalade

Directions

1. Sprinkle some salt and pepper over the loin chops. Coat them with a cooking spray.
2. Place a large pan over high heat. Cook in it the chops for 1 min on each side.
3. Stir in the grape juice. Place over it the marmalade and put on the lid.
4. Let them cook for 3 to 4 min on each side. Serve them hot.
5. Enjoy..

Cast
Iron Sweet Potatoes

Prep Time: 10 mins
Total Time: 50 mins

Servings per Recipe: 4
Calories	340.4 kcal
Fat	7.1 g
Cholesterol	0.0 mg
Sodium	21.2 mg
Carbohydrates	66.6 g
Protein	3.8 g

Ingredients

2 tbsp olive oil
2 lbs. yams, peeled and cut into pieces
1 onion, chopped
1 serrano pepper, seeded and chopped
2 tbsp ginger, chop
3 tbsp lime juice

2 tbsp parsley, chopped
salt and pepper

Directions

1. Place a large pan over high heat. Heat in it the oil. Cook in it the yams for 11 min.
2. Stir in the onion, serrano pepper, and ginger. Lower the heat and cook them for 8 to 9 min.
3. Stir in the lime juice with parsley, a pinch of salt and pepper. Serve your yams skillet hot.
4. Enjoy..

PAPAYA
Lampur

Prep Time: 10 mins
Total Time: 35 mins

Servings per Recipe: 4	
Calories	252.1 kcal
Fat	11.2 g
Cholesterol	100.8 mg
Sodium	44.3 mg
Carbohydrates	35.7 g
Protein	5.2 g

Ingredients

2 ripe papayas, halved and seeded
2 pieces stem ginger in syrup, drained
and cut into matchsticks
8 amaretti cookies, crushed
3 tbsp raisins
1 lime, juice and chopped zest

1/4 C. chopped pistachios
1 tbsp light muscovado sugar
4 tbsp heavy cream

Directions

1. Reserve 1 tbsp of ginger syrup.
2. Before you do anything, preheat the oven to 400 F.
3. Get a mixing bowl: Stir in it the amaretti with raisins, ginger, lime juice, lime zest, and two-thirds of the nuts.
4. Mix in 4 tbsp of cream and sugar to make the filling.
5. Place the papaya halves in a baking pan. Drizzle the remaining syrup on top.
6. Spoon the filling over the papayas. Top them with the remaining nuts.
7. Place the pan in the oven and let them cook for 26 min.
8. Serve your glazed papayas with some ice cream.
9. Enjoy..

Kyoto
Sauce

🍜 Prep Time: 15 mins
🕐 Total Time: 45 mins

Servings per Recipe: 1
Calories	255.9 kcal
Fat	7.0 g
Cholesterol	0.0 mg
Sodium	3743.3 mg
Carbohydrates	39.2 g
Protein	5.9 g

Ingredients

1/2 oz. ginger, peeled, cut in pieces
1 small shallot, peeled, cut in pieces
1 garlic clove, peeled
3/4 C. white vinegar
3/4 C. low sodium soy sauce
1/4 C. seasoned rice vinegar
2 tbsp dark molasses

1 1/2 tbsp wasabi paste, see note
1 tbsp brown sugar, packed
1 tbsp sesame oil
1 1/2 tsp powdered ginger
1/2 tsp ground black pepper

Directions

1. Get a blender: Put in it the ginger, shallot and garlic. Blend them smooth.
2. Pour in the rest of the ingredients. Blend them smooth.
3. Pour the wasabi into a jar and seal it. Place it in the fridge until ready to use.
4. Enjoy.

NOTE: To make wasabi paste combine 3 tsps of store bought wasabi powder with 1 tsp of water. Stir the mix until it is smooth, add more water if needed.

TUSCAN
Biscotti

Prep Time: 15 mins
Total Time: 50 mins

Servings per Recipe: 24
Calories	137.0 kcal
Fat	7.0 g
Cholesterol	28.2 mg
Sodium	84.2 mg
Carbohydrates	16.3 g
Protein	2.5 g

Ingredients

2 C. all-purpose flour
1 1/2 tsp baking powder
1 tsp ground ginger
1/4 tsp salt
2/3 C. sugar
1/2 C. butter, softened

2 large eggs
1 tsp vanilla extract
2/3 C. crystallized ginger, chopped
1/2 C. blanched almond, sliced, toasted
1/2 C. white chocolate chips

Directions

1. Before you do anything, preheat the oven to 325 F.
2. Coat a baking pan with some butter and flour.
3. Get a mixing bowl: Stir in it the flour, baking powder, ground ginger and salt.
4. Get a large mixing bowl: Cream in it the eggs with vanilla until they become pale.
5. Add the flour mix gradually while mixing all the time.
6. Fold the crystallized ginger, almonds and white chocolate chips into the mixture.
7. Shape the dough into two 12 inches logs. Lay them on the greased baking pan.
8. Cook them in the oven for 26 to 32 min until they become golden brown.
9. Remove the pan from the heat and let them rest for 6 min. Slice them into 1 inch thick slices.
10. Place the slices back on the baking pan. Cook them in the oven for 11 to 13 min.
11. Allow everything to cool down completely. Serve them with some tea.
12. Enjoy..

Oriental
Ginger Tuna Steaks

Prep Time: 15 mins
Total Time: 23 mins

Servings per Recipe: 4

Calories	854.7 kcal
Fat	61.3 g
Cholesterol	242.0 mg
Sodium	720.6 mg
Carbohydrates	11.3 g
Protein	64.2 g

Ingredients

36 oz. ahi tuna steaks
2 tbsp olive oil
ground pepper
3 tbsp butter
1/3 C. green onion
2 tbsp ginger, grated
4 garlic cloves pressed
8 oz. shiitake mushrooms, sliced

2 tbsp soy sauce
1 1/2 C. whipping cream
3 tbsp lime juice, squeezed
1/4 C. cilantro
6 C. baby greens
3 C. wasabi mashed potatoes
cilantro

Directions

1. Season the steaks with some salt and pepper.
2. Place a large pan over high heat. Heat in it the oil. Sear them for 3 to 4 min on each side.
3. Drain the steaks and place them aside.
4. Stir the butter, onion, ginger and garlic in the same pan. Cook them for 1 min.
5. Stir in the mushroom and cook them for 3 min. Stir in the cream with soy sauce. Cook them for 2 min.
6. Stir in the lime juice with cilantro, a pinch of salt and pepper.
7. Enjoy..

SIMPLE
Homemade Red Curry Paste (Thailand Style)

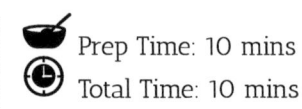

Prep Time: 10 mins
Total Time: 10 mins

Servings per Recipe: 1

Calories	300.4
Fat	3.5 g
Cholesterol	0 mg
Sodium	2368.8 mg
Carbohydrates	71.1 g
Protein	7.5 g

Ingredients

1/4 C. chopped scallion
1/4 C. chopped fresh cilantro
2 tbsps minced garlic
2 tbsps grated fresh gingerroot
1 tbsp freshly grated lemon rinds
1 tbsp brown sugar
1-2 fresh red chilies or 1-2 green chili, minced

3 tbsps fresh lemon juice
1 tbsp ground coriander
1 tsp turmeric
1/2 tsp salt

Directions

1. Add the following your food processor: scallion, cilantro, garlic, ginger root, lemons / lime, brown sugar, chilies, lemon / lime juice, coriander, turmeric, and salt.
2. Process and pulse everything until it becomes a smooth paste.
3. Enjoy.

NOTES: To prepare a red curry paste use red chilies for a green curry paste use green chilies.

Plum-Ginger Chutney

🥣 Prep Time: 20 mins

🕐 Total Time: 1 hr 10 mins

Servings per Recipe: 5

Calories	567.7 kcal
Fat	1.0 g
Cholesterol	0.0 mg
Sodium	1190.1 mg
Carbohydrates	142.6 g
Protein	2.4 g

Ingredients

3 1/2 C. purple plums, seeds removed
1 C. brown sugar
1 C. sugar
3/4 C. cider vinegar
1 C. golden raisins
2 tsps salt
1/3 C. chopped onion

1 clove garlic, minced
2 tsps mustard seeds
3 tbsps chopped crystallized ginger
3/4 tsp cayenne

Directions

1. In a large nonreactive pan, mix together vinegar and sugar and bring to a boil.
2. Cook, stirring continuously till sugar is dissolved completely.
3. Stir in the remaining ingredients and bring to a boil.
4. Reduce the heat to low and cook, stirring occasionally for about 40-50 minutes or till desired thickness of chutney.
5. Transfer the chutney into hot sterilized jars and seal tightly and keep aside to cool.
6. For better taste use after about 1 month..

CAJUN
Seasoning

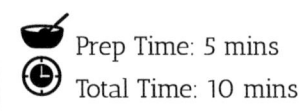
Prep Time: 5 mins
Total Time: 10 mins

Servings per Recipe: 12
Calories	19.5 kcal
Fat	0.5 g
Cholesterol	0.0 mg
Sodium	200.8 mg
Carbohydrates	4.0 g
Protein	0.9 g

Ingredients

5 tbsp paprika
2 tbsp garlic powder
1 tbsp black pepper
1 tbsp ground red pepper
1 tbsp white pepper
1 tbsp thyme

1 tbsp oregano
1 tsp salt
1 tsp chili powder
1 tsp onion powder

Directions

1. Get a small mixing bowl: Mix in it all the ingredients. Place it in the storing jar then use it whenever your desire.
2. Enjoy..

Printed in Great Britain
by Amazon

55356685R00057